Law and Religion

by
Timothy L. Fort

McFarland & Company, Inc., Publishers
Jefferson, North Carolina, and London

3-88

Library of Congress Cataloguing-in-Publication Data

Fort, Timothy L., 1958–
Law and religion.

Bibliography: p. 127
Includes index.
1. Law — United States — Religious aspects.
2. Religion and state — United States.
3. United States — Religion.
I. Title.
BL65.L33F67   1987   261.5   86-33735

ISBN 0-89950-265-2 (sewn softcover; acid-free natural paper)

Printed in the United States of America.

McFarland   Box 611   Jefferson NC 28640

To Mom and Dad
and in memory of Aunt Phud

Table of Contents

vii

Introduction

This book proposes to clarify the connection of law and religion by muddling it. In a strange, but true way, it is only by muddling it that we can begin to put some sense into the connection, a connection which is important generally for society and important for America currently because of renewed debates about the role of religion in politics and the separation of church and state.

The contemporary debate of religion and law and the related debates of religion and politics and church and state is running dangerously close to what is popularly known as a zero-sum game; a game in which the only benefit that one side can achieve is directly related to a corresponding loss by the other side. Thus, positions become even more rigid. Either one is proabortion or antiabortion, proprayer in school or antiprayer in school, propornography or antipornography. In many cases, one is categorized as religious or a-religious. This book does not attempt to address the particular merits of these issues, but instead, on a more abstract level, attempts to understand the philosophical and theological connection of law and religion, the historical distortions resulting from inadequately accounting for religion, and a particular historical example showing that religion and law are related on a much deeper level than has been often recognized.

The thesis of this book is that law and religion are expressions of a way of life and since they are both a part of life, they are always connected with one another. On a philosophical basis, both law and religion are ethics. Ethics are not simply decisions of what is

1

right and wrong, but are an entire expression of who we are as persons, what values we have, what is important to us, what are appropriate ways to act, and what other ordering processes we employ to make sense out of human existence. This ordering process occurs both in religion where ethics are developed based on daily human existence and metaphysics, and in law where ethics are also developed based on daily human existence, and at least some common philosophical, if not metaphysical, assumptions. Law really is secular ethics and morality really is religious ethics.

Because they are ethical parts of life, and because of their historical dependence, they are heavily indebted to one another. Separating them from one another, or blithely equating each with their most prominent institutional manifestations (law with the state and religion with the church) is extremely misleading. But, those misleading equations are the normal Western understanding of law and religion. Unscrambling the equations can cause great confusion for us because we are so used to thinking that religion and law are separate. They are not separate. However, connecting them does not necessarily lead either to a church-dictated law or a state-dictated religion. Part I of this book describes two promising theories of the relation of law and religion and then builds upon those theories to exposit a third theory based on law and religion being ethical ways of life.

Part II analyzes major American legal historians to see how they have dealt with the connection of law and religion. Overwhelmingly, they have fallen into the trap of equating religion with the institutional church. The general theory they propose is that the power of religion ended around the time of the American Revolution as the industrial revolution hit the continent with full force. Since then, they argue, American legal history has been the story of economic power and efficiency.

The deepest problem with this theory is that the dominant faith in America, Calvinism, expressed in a variety of forms, remained intact with virtually the same values as it possessed prior to the American Revolution. Calvinism, which embraced financial success as a sign of God's favor, was very sympathetic to the industrial revolution. To be sure, some of the moral crimes condemned by the Puritans were more sparingly prosecuted and the

Puritan churches were disestablished; however, religion, based on values, beliefs, and ethics, was very much a leader in the development of the industrial revolution. By ignoring religion as an active constituent in American legal history, these historians have greatly contributed to the confusing thought that what is economic is religion-free and that economic laws are also religion-free. But since laws are dependent upon deep societal values, laws are connected to religion. The legal historians contribute to a profound problem of Americans looking at their laws apart from the laws' deepest values.

Part III uses an early nineteenth century example of the connection of law and religion in the judicial system. Connecticut Supreme Court justices Tapping Reeve and Zephania Swift presided at a time when the Congregational Church of Connecticut was being disestablished and at a time when religious diversity was being experienced for the first time in the state's history. Although the particular theologies of both men differed, both men were profoundly aware of their deeply felt religiousness. Both, in varying degrees, welcomed the changes occurring in Connecticut and both led the development of scientific jurisprudence. This was an attempt to bring methods to adjudication that would legitimately appeal to its diverse religious population but would also perpetuate the lessons and laws of Puritan Connecticut.

These men were very aware that religion and law were connected, but they developed a jurisprudence which was more broadly based than a jurisprudence from a single religious perspective. Their jurisprudence took into account the different religions of their times. As is common in American history, these men perpetuated the religious nature of American law but did so by limiting religious prejudices and stretching legal concepts. They were faithful to their sacred ethics but were also able to embrace others by their secular ethics. Part III does not argue that exact instances of Connecticut's experience are replicated everywhere in American history, but it does stand for the proposition that the method of looking at judges may be expanded to see if Connecticut's experience is replicated, and that American law and religion might be often connected in terms that avoid church-dictated law or state-dictated religion.

A few personal comments are in order before proceeding to the main text of the book. This book was actually written in reverse order. Part III was first written as part of a senior thesis in law school, when I was also completing a graduate degree in systematic theology. During my studies for my law and theology degrees, I was continually impressed by the similarity in the learning method and in the objectives of the subject matter. At the time I began my thesis, I began with little more than the belief that there was something similar between the two fields. In researching Connecticut history, the connection became clearer as the Connecticut judges expressed what they were doing in their jurisprudence.

Having seen this connection in a specific historical context, my attention turned to see if other historians had also confronted the same connection. Seeing that they did not, and seeing why they had not, I turned to scholars who had attempted to explain the connection in terms other than traditional scholastic natural law theology. This research prompted Parts I and II.

Part IV is an attempt to show how the modern debate between the fundamentalists and the moderate traditionalists, as exemplified by Jerry Falwell and Mario Cuomo respectively, is a continuation of the debate concerning law and religion, and whether sacred and secular ethics are, or should be, linked together and what role they have in our society.

The story of the writing of the book is not simply repeated to reminisce but rather to illustrate that the book was written because of the realization that there was a connection that contemporary Americans have often missed. The modern separation of law and religion simply confuses social/religious debates in the political and legal sphere. These debates are bound to become even more controversial, bitter, and divisive if participants dig into their intransigent positions. The argument that religion should be completely kept out of law is unreasonable, for as this book argues, religion and law will always be connected.

Attempting to keep religion out of law only serves to obscure the real values behind the political arguments. At the same time, arguing for religion to be reintroduced into politics often is the same as arguing that the "other side" is not religious, or perhaps more diplomatically, is not interested in values. This results in an arrogance of moral superiority which may be more dangerous than keeping religion out of politics. It would seem more sensible to recognize that both sides of the argument are entitled to respect and that the way out of the bitter polemics is to devise a method which can appeal to both sides, as Tapping Reeve and Zephania Swift did for nineteenth century Connecticut.

After reading the book, the reader's mind may be where my mind was after beginning the Connecticut section, namely, that there seems to be a connection between law and religion, but that one is not sure what the connection is. In part for that reason, I have kept this book quite short. Few things are as confusing as a new approach which continues for hundreds of pages. I would rather the reader end this book with a very unsettled, or even angry feeling and then go back through it to get used to its ideas than to give up half-way through, or continue to half-heartedly read the remainder of the book, forgetting what the points were of the earlier chapters. If this book seems occasionally disjointed it may well be that the argument is strange enough to take some getting used to.

I have struggled to keep this book free of technical terms. Given the fact that both law and theology are ancient fields which are overburdened with insiders' terminology, this has been a very difficult task. Yet, I did not see much point in writing a book about theology which a lawyer may not understand, nor did I see much point in writing a legal book that a theologian may not understand. More importantly, I did not want to bury a layperson with the technical terms of both law and theology. A trained reader in either field may find my explanations too simple or too awkward, but that has usually been the result of trying to avoid complicated terminology.

Finally, this book is intended neither as a complete exposition of the connection of law and religion nor as an attack on anyone named in the book, or with those who may agree with people named in the book. It is meant to be an introduction into a way of working ourselves out of a potentially dangerous debate and it criticizes only because I feel that past theories may not help us out in this modern debate. The modern debate of religion and law, church and state, religion and politics needs new, tolerant insights. This book is an introductory attempt to provide a philosophical and historical framework for some new insights.

PART I
CONNECTING LAW
AND RELIGION

1. The Mutual Dependence

Harold Berman and
"The Interaction of Law and Religion" (1974)

The first question to be asked is how religion and law are related. For modern Americans, this is a difficult question because Americans generally like to keep church separated from state and therefore also like to keep religion separated from law. While understandable, this attitude confuses the issue, because religion is not necessarily identical to the church, and law is not necessarily identical to the state. Instead of simply repeating the standard rhetoric that church and state should have no business with each other, it is important to see how religion and law are connected.

Is law a weapon of governmental coercion, is it some natural, omnipresent state of right and wrong, is it simply the custom of the people, is it a game played and manipulated by rational technicians such as judges and lawyers? At the risk of totally conceding the discussion to semantics, the definition one uses for law will largely determine law's strengths and weaknesses and in turn will require differing roles for religion.

If law is simply the dictates of the state, whether by legislative, executive, or judicial action, law loses nearly all sense of justice, and unless the rulers are backed by a powerful military force, law will have little effectiveness. Similarly, if law becomes a game played, manipulated, and only understood by legal technicians, the people will feel helpless and quite likely oppressed by a system which seems to have little responsiveness to societal needs. This oppressive feeling may exist even if the legal technicians really do operate for societal benefit because the people will be unable to comprehend and appreciate it.

If law is something universal, divine and omnipresent, one must struggle with historic situations in which laws may in some instances be fair and in others unfair. One must also learn to recognize this natural law as it is limited to or crosses traditional religious or philosophical lines.

Finally, if law is simply societal custom, one misses the dynamic of how custom changes. More importantly, this view of the law ignores the power of changes in the law, even in a democratic society where government acts in violation of custom. America's civil rights legislation in the 1960s certainly did not connect with a great deal of customary consensus, particularly in the South, yet not only did it become law, it has become reasonably successful.

These different theories of law carry with them different appropriate criticisms. The theory used will determine criticisms that law will encounter. The same problem exists in defining religion.

Many identify religion with the church, which itself is a mistake, but even if the identification was proper, definitional problems would exist. Does the "church" mean an institutional body with a recognizable, established leadership, visible organizations, rules of membership conduct, and defined alliances and allegiances? Is the church an activist political entity, or is it monastic community? Is the church a broader group of people who are personally connected with God? (For an excellent breakdown of the types of churches within Christianity, see Avery Dulles' *Models of the Church* and Richard Niebuhr's *Christ and Culture*.)

The point may be carried to religion also, but the idea should be clear that in defining religion and law, a great many things are immediately decided. It is too easy, and too deceiving, to simply understand the interaction of law and religion as the relationship of church and state. What needs to be done is to understand anew religion and law.

If we are to understand the connection of law and religion, we should begin with Harold Berman. In two major books and in numerous articles, Berman has argued that law and religion need one another in order to prosper. Berman believes that

> Law without (what I call) religion degenerates into a mechanical legalism. Religion without (what I call) law loses its social effectiveness.[1]

Berman tentatively defines law as structures and processes of allocations of rights and duties within a society which applies religious intuitions and commitments to practical daily dealings with other human beings. He defines religion as society's intuitions of and commitments to ultimate meaning and the purpose of life.[2] Berman's approach will lead to a distinction between religion as theology and law as ethics.

Berman analyzes the interaction of law and religion by first examining the religious dimension of law. In so doing he deepens his definition of both law and religion.

> Law is not only a body of rules; it is people legislating, adjudicating, administering, negotiating — it is a living process of allocating rights and duties and thereby resolving conflicts and creating channels of cooperation. Religion is not only a set of doctrines and exercises, it is people manifesting a collective concern for the ultimate meaning and purpose of life — it is a shared intuition of and commitment to transcendent values.[3]

If law is this living process of people relating to others, and religion focuses on the ultimate meaning of life, where is the connection between the two other than by both being aspects of social experience? Berman answers that the common basis of law and religion are symbols that attempt to grasp a truth beyond mere human existence. Symbols exist in various forms, and Berman identifies four characteristics that religion and law share. For instance, legal rituals

> . . . symbolize (bring into being) the fundamental postulate of all legal systems, even the most rudimentary, that like cases should be decided alike; they raise that postulate from a matter of intellectual perception and moral duty to a matter of collective faith.[4]

Before looking at the four characteristics shared by law and religion, it is very important to understand what Berman means by symbol in this context. A symbol is not simply an abstract concept which mirrors reality, but it is a representative act which reinforces the values and reality of the act. A rather rudimentary athletic analogy might illustrate the idea of a symbol effectively.

It is often said that football is like the game of life. In football, one must learn to prepare for important events, must learn to bounce back from disappointment, must play within the rules, and must cooperate with other team members in order to achieve victory. The player also learns about competition both within the team where competition is healthy, but must be contained in order to preserve cooperation of the team, and against another team where competition can be more fierce. All of these aspects of football have counterparts in real life and so they may be said to symbolize life. However, the symbols of football are not meaningless, neutral mirrors of life. By competing, the player does not simply learn that competition exists in life; instead, the spirit of competition within him is developed and is applied to football as well as life. Cooperation is developed which carries over into life. By picking oneself up after defeat, one brings into being the value of perseverance. Football, then, does not simply imitate life, but develops the values of life by its very existence. The issue of religion and law is a good deal more serious than football but the same understanding of symbol nevertheless applies. Not only do the rituals of law imitate values of fair trials, but by their very existence, the rituals of law develop the conceptions of fair trials.

Religion and law both use symbols to grasp a truth greater than human existence. In addition to ritual, religion and law both share the characteristics of tradition, authority, and the universality of concepts. The traditional aspect, for instance, is reflected by the idea of precedent. Precedent is a predictable identifiable part of law which shapes and is shaped by community values. Berman expresses the religious aspect of this by saying

> The law need not be eternal, but it also must not be arbitrary, and therefore it must change by reinterpreting what has been done before. The traditional aspect of law, its sense of ongoingness, cannot be explained in purely secular and rational terms, since it embodies man's concept of time, which itself it [sic] bound up with the transrational and with religion.[5]

Law and religion both must deal with the ongoingness and relevance of tradition. Thus, tradition is a characteristic of both law and religion and links the two.

Having connected law and religion by the common characteristics of ritual, tradition, and authority, Berman says that law becomes ineffective when it is divorced from religion.

> In the last analysis, what deters crime is the tradition of being law-abiding and this in turn depends upon a deeply or passionately held conviction that law is not only an instrument of secular policy but also part of the ultimate purpose and meaning of life.[6]

This is a belief that the principles of both law and religion apply to humanity generally, or at least apply in some culturally adjusted form. While all people may not share a specific theological or legal doctrine, the general concept applies to anyone. This position, to which Jacques Ellul (see Chapter 2) will strenuously object, links all humans to a common purpose of meaning within life: a religious belief. Without its legitimizing higher truths, law is too weak to create solutions for the societal problems because "[L]aw without faith degenerates into legalism; this indeed is what is happening in many parts of America and of the Western world."[7,8] The allocation of rights and duties must be guided by society's intuitions of the ultimate meaning of life if these rights and duties are to be respected.

Berman may well be correct in insisting that law and religion must be related to each other if both are to flourish, but there remains the question of whether Berman has not excessively limited both law and religion by his definitions. As long as he can keep law and religion separate but related, his analysis is very helpful; the conceptual separation of law and religion often leads to the identification of religion with institutional religion and of law to the state.

Perhaps Berman's best analysis, and certainly his most exhaustive work in the field of law and religion, is in describing the influence of Christianity on Western law. It is also here that any writer in the field of law and religion is on perilous territory for it is extremely easy to equate the institutional Christian church with all religion. This is particularly tempting because of the pervasive-

ness of the Christian church in Western society. The institutional
Christian church has certainly influenced many aspects of Western
history, but it must be remembered that Christianity is far more
complex than the institutional church. The institutional church
has been a jewel of Christianity as well as an embarrassment.
While it is legitimate to recognize the influence of the institutional
church, one cannot ignore the deeper aspects of Christianity. Berman does not confuse the two, but the confusion is so easily made
that it is important to remember the distinction.

Berman argues that the Papal Revolution of the late eleventh
and early twelfth centuries established the first modern legal
system. (For an exhaustive treatment of the Papal Revolution and
its impact on secular law, see Berman's *Law and Revolution.*) The
Papal Revolution created a visible, hierarchical church with its
own system of law. Secular law imitated the new canon law so that
the canon law and the new secular law sought to reconcile conflicts
by analysis and synthesis.[9] This synthesized law was thought to be
more humane because it was not arbitrary, capricious, or
violent.[10] The result, however, was a conflict between secular and
ecclesiastical authorities as both claimed jurisdiction over the same
things. Unlike ancient Israel, where there was no distinction between the state and the church, medieval folks were caught in a
battle between the church and the emerging states.

Of deeper significance than the institutional influence was the
influence of Christian values on the new law. Berman argues that
the medieval church taught the principle of the growth of the law,
a principle which carried over to the secular law and which certainly has carried down to American society.[11] This principle
taught that law was not a stagnant mass, but that human law continually developed and changed. More importantly, the Protestant
Reformation's emphasis on the individual led to the developing
laws of contract and property.[12] Once Luther made the relationship between the individual and God primary, the individual's
relationship with all other people and things took on new importance. Instead of simply viewing a human as a person who would
remain in an identical status throughout life and interact with
others only consistent with society's for that status, the law of contract gradually expanded to the point where the individual could

participate in transactions even if those transactions seemed to be against the person's best interests. The primacy of the individual also gave rise to each person's right to own property and to do with it as the person pleased.

Berman also notes two other Christian principles of great importance. He states that Congregational Calvinism produced the idea of the social contract and of government by the consent of the governed.[13] Of course this principle was closely tied to the developing importance of the individual since individuals were contracting to be bound together and were consenting to be governed.

Finally, Berman notes that one of the most important principles of the American and French revolutions was the idea of the right of civil disobedience.[14] This principle was based on the idea that while secular government was to be respected, each Christian had an overriding duty to be faithful to the law of God. If a time came when one could not be loyal to God by being loyal to the secular government, one had to be disobedient to the state.

With the coming of the Enlightenment, religion was gradually reduced to a private affair. The belief in abilities of humans took precedence over the belief in God. Christian values, however, were not abandoned but were largely assumed by liberal democracies in the West.[15] Thus, even though the role and the power of the institutional Christian church was not as great after the Enlightenment as it was before the Enlightenment, the values of Christianity remained powerful and shaped the laws of modern Western democracies.

Berman effectively stays away from identifying religion with institutions because he recognizes that religious values continued to be powerful even after the power of the church was diminished. There is great danger in equating religion with institutions as is so often done because religious institutions are notoriously slow in recognizing the concerns of the faithful. Prior to Luther, the Renaissance popes were often attacked for their disregard of the importance of their sacred office, but these popes nevertheless continued to mock the papal office. (See Barbara Tuchman's *The March of Folly*.)

The Roman Catholic church had similar difficulties prior to Vatican II because it had started to become irrelevant to its faithful. The Congregational Church of Connecticut was nearly paralyzed with fear when political pressure forced the disestablishment of this state church, only to discover that a stronger church emerged by addressing itself directly to the concerns of the people in a noncoercive way.

Religious institutions may be concerned with religious sources, but they remain institutions. As institutions, they are prone to the same problems which any institution may have such as unresponsiveness, bureaucratic inefficiency, and self-preservation even where that spirit of self-preservation may be counterproductive to the faith the institution professes. Because it is an institution, the church is only partially instructive of the religion of the people. To be sure, the church is probably the most important reservoir for understanding the values of a given people in Western society, but one must remember that the church, like the state, may also often miss the religious concerns of its constituents. Historically, religious institutions may have been more powerful than they are now, but the level of their institutional powerfulness may be more dependent upon factors other than religious faith.

As a final part of Berman's analysis, he examines the legal dimension of religion. This does not mean the legal rights of the institutional church, but of the need for law as an aspect of religion. Berman states that

> The divorce of law from love rests on the misconception that the essence of law consists in its rules and that law may be defined, essentially, as a body of rules. This neglects the active, living qualities of law as a process of social ordering.... Law is not only rules and concepts; law is also, and primarily, a set of relationships among people.[16]

It is a mistake, therefore, to view law as a creation of the state or even as a creation of a sacred institution. Law seems closer to an idea of ethics, of applying the religious (as defined by Berman) understanding of a society to the events and personalities of human life. This law, or ethics, in turn provides an atmosphere in which society's intuitions (religion) develop and flourish:

> [legal rules] are necessary to protect our unique, individual per-
> sonalities from capricious, arbitrary, and oppressive actions . . . our
> personalities require — for love's sake — the protection of general
> principles impartially administered.[17]

Thus the chief justification for law is to create conditions in which
love will flourish.[18]

Berman's analysis stops just one step short of the analysis
which will be more fully developed in Chapter 4. Berman is saying
that society needs both religion and law because society must have
a collective intuition and commitment to shared beliefs in the
ultimate reason for existence, and that these intuitions and commitments must be the basis for legal application. In truth, all law
(as defined by Berman) must have religion if it is to win any type
of common support, and all religion (as defined by Berman) must
have law if it is to avoid a neutral mysticism. Together, law and
religion amount to a total way of life in which metaphysics and
ethics are mutually dependent. Emphasizing separate aspects of
such a way of life may emphasize the components, but it also leads
to a temptation to repeat the mistakes of Western analysis.

Once one has separated law and religion, there is a strong
temptation to focus on the components instead of the whole. Thus,
societal intuitions are emphasized at the expense of understanding
what those intuitions mean in a practical sense, thereby leading to
ineffective mysticism; and ethical applications are emphasized at
the expense of understanding the grounding sources of these
ethics, which lead to bland, ineffective, and mechanical legal-
isms.

Breaking law and religion into separate components also leads
toward the identification of each with the institution with which
they are commonly associated. Law is normally identified with the
state, and therefore the state lends to law a sense of religion-free
rules. But no rules which are popularly followed are devoid of
religious content, so that the actual religious sources from which
the laws emanate become obscured. By attempting to avoid
religious prejudices, religious values are obscured and laws lose
their authority.

Likewise religion is normally identified with the institutional church. But the church is often unable to account for all the religious values of its own congregation, let alone the values of the society. Religion then becomes identified with an institutional body that itself is struggling for its own preservation, a preservation that in a religiously diverse society is bound to impinge upon other religious institutions. Religion then rides on the same level as special interest groups in politics.

Berman's analysis effectively addresses the needs of any given society, but his definitions are really not decisively helpful in understanding the contemporary problems of how a pluralistic society, such as the United States, can identify and create law which is effective because of the underlying religious values, when the religions of the society are so diverse. How can a religious institution provide the basis for societal law when the very basis will conflict with another religious institution? In short, the question that can be posed to all Americans is the religious-legal question: How can people maintain their meaningful identity with their particular religion while simultaneously uniting with other religions to create effective law? The analysis of Jacques Ellul's work will provide some answers to this, and Chapter 4 will attempt to address the remainder of the question.

2. The Purist Approach

Jacques Ellul and
"The Theological Foundation of Law" (1960)

How are Americans who live in a religiously diverse country to deal with other faiths when creating law? To many, the legitimate answer is to firmly anchor oneself in one's own religion, be as purely faithful to that religion as is possible, and to limit cooperation with other faiths. This purist tendency has deep roots in United States history. Undoubtedly, the most famous example of this tendency was the Pilgrims who came to America to purely practice their faith, uncontaminated by English belief. The purist approach requires a firm, confident belief that one's beliefs are truly God's way, and that the faith is superior to other faiths. While the purist approach can often lead to intolerant behavior, it is an approach which projects a great deal of strength.

Jacques Ellul's *The Theological Foundation of Law* exemplifies the purist approach, although Ellul, a Frenchman, is not directly applying the purist approach to American pluralism. However, Ellul's approach is quite similar to many purists throughout American history, both in religious content and in justification of the pluralist perspective.

Where Harold Berman separated law and religion in order to define each, Jacques Ellul's religion swallows law. Ellul's faith consists of a basic Calvinist understanding of God, humanity, and government. Using that understanding, he uncompromisingly insists that all law emanates from his religion.

Ellul's concern is to understand God's will and to analyze institutions in light of God's will; he does not first look at what an institution is doing and then attempt to provide justification for its
history. Ellul believes that God is not an aloof creator who now
neutrally observes human affairs, but who is actively involved in
all human history.[1] In other words, Ellul completely rejects the notion, influential in America, of a deistic God.

Ellul is concerned with natural law as are most theologians
who write about jurisprudence, but his understanding of natural
law is radically different from other natural law theorists. Ellul's
primary objection of natural law theories is that they inap-
propriately attempt to provide a meeting gound for Christians and
non–Christians.[2] Underlying natural law theories is a notion that
God's law is imprinted upon humans simply by their existence as
humans and that while Christians may have superior sources to
identify God's law, all humans are able to recognize it. Instead of
viewing natural law as a theory which links all humans to God,
Ellul understands natural law to be a specific event in history, a
certain stage within a community's development. He develops the
foundation for his natural law theory by an excellent four-part
typology of the development of law.

Ellul argues that in its origin law is religious. Law is an expression of the will of a god as that will is formulated by a priest,
and is given religious approval with ritual. Moving from this
stage, law gradually becomes more secular as the state power
separates from the religious power. It is at this juncture that
natural law occurs. Law is established by custom or legislation independent of the religious power of the society as if it were the
spontaneous creation of economic, political, and moral factors. It
springs directly from within society from common sentiment and
is the expression of the conscience of the people. In this stage, there
is a general consensus of what is right and wrong, appropriate and
inappropriate. In this stage, law neither is dictated by the state nor
by religious institution, but by the common conscience of the
people.

Stage three appears as law becomes explained, interpreted
and rationally theorized. This stage, which Ellul compares to
fourth century B.C. Greece, first century B.C. Rome, and

eighteenth century England and Germany, features the first attempt of legal theorists to make law an object of understanding
rather than a spontaneous application of the values of the society.
Stage four then occurs when law becomes solely the creation of the
state. Principles are announced by theorists of the state and
juridical technique becomes increasingly precise as jurists attempt
to apply the principles of the law in a rational, logical manner. At
this point, law has become a game, a game based on the
systematic, logical application of principles to the case at hand.
Since it is an object, however, it can be controlled by whomever
has the control of the state. The state may announce the principles
and appoint the jurists who will tailor their method to be consistent
with the demands of those who control the state.[3]

Ellul is not optimistic about the results of the rejection of
natural law. He believes that once law has become a matter of
juridical technique, there will be continued technical proliferation
unless there is some human or natural counterweight. Once law is
truly in the control of the state, no counterweight exists, as was the
case with Naziism and Communism. Once this state of affairs is
reached, law gradually ceases to be observed and respected so that
the only way for the law to be enforced is through police measures
Further, Ellul does not believe that there is anything that humans
can do to correct the situation for only God can return society to
natural law. This moribund state of affairs raises the question
of what Ellul really means by law and what he means by human
law in particular, for Ellul has understandings of law as a part of
human society, and also has an idea of what law really is. He
underscores the distinction by analyzing both divine law and
human law.

Because of Ellul's Calvinist underpinnings, it is not surprising
that his understanding of law becomes completely identified with
God's law as articulated by scripture. God's, or divine, law is
always an expression of justice and righteousness in scripture. In
light of God's justice, Ellul argues that all human justice is unjust
simply because human justice is not bound up with mercy and
forgiveness. God's righteousness is Jesus Christ. Jesus was God's
fullest expression of mercy and forgiveness, and since the divine
law is mercy and forgiveness, Jesus, the personal embodiment of

mercy and forgiveness, becomes the divine law. All righteousness, then, must be connected to Jesus Christ.[4]

The difficulty in Ellul's argument is that it gives little guidance to humans. While Ellul may be correct, and it is this author's belief that, with modifications, he is correct, he reduces the human ability to act to meaninglessness because he stresses God's activity. Humans simply can do nothing but act out God's will, they are not responsible participants in the development of God's kingdom. This approach produces three negative results.

First, the lack of human responsibility tempts humans to disregard the importance of their own activities. Since, in the end, it is God who is controlling all action, it is less important for humans to become actively responsible for doing God's work. This state of affairs always tempts decadence, which will itself eliminate the respected legal order needed for God's speaking in society.

Second, Ellul's arguments simply miss the rationality of post–Enlightenment times, which is a belief in the ability of human solutions to produce at least some effective results. Because Ellul essentially removes human responsibility from the legal process, there is little chance that his argument can be accepted in a Western country. Ellul may not be concerned about such an acceptance, but the fact remains that humans will be concerned about law and religion and will try to improve upon present law and religion whether or not Ellul says that they really are doing anything. Therefore, the need that has to be addressed is what should guide constant human actions in law and religion.

Third, Ellul's argument becomes religiously specific in a way that, oddly, does not leave room for Christian humility and for God's continuing activity. It is strange that Ellul, who has such a low opinion of human nature, should not be similarly humble in sketching his religious and legal philosophy. He argues for a very specific vision of Jesus which may or may not encompass all that Jesus was and is, and he rather routinely rejects the notion that non–Christians have the ability to develop secular law. He thereby essentially limits Jesus' revelation to his earthly life and our interpretation of it. For a theologian who stresses God's continual activity in daily human life, it is strange that he does not allow for Jesus to be active among people who are not admirers of the

Christian interpretation of Jesus' earthly existence. Ellul himself gets caught in the trap of institutional religion in which Jesus ceases to be a dynamic presence in daily life; religion instead becomes the logical extension of Jesus' earthly life. In a sense, such an interpretation of Jesus fits Ellul's stages three and four in his typology where Jesus' life and teachings become rationally and systematically interpreted rather than being an ingrained way of living.

Thus, Ellul's argument, while it is quite useful, also runs into some severe problems when applying it in today's society. The source of his Christocentricism is itself debatable, his solution tempts decadence since it diminishes human responsibility, and he misses the practical need to provide guidance for contemporary Christians.

The purist approach is compelling for it focuses energy solely upon faithfulness to a conception of God's will. Law which conflicts with this conception must therefore be changed, rejected, or ignored. This conception, which Berman recognizes as the principle of civil disobedience, is strong because the requirements of the purist approach are normally clear. Ultimately, however, the purist approach may be challenged by questioning whether it is truly and humbly open to its own assertion of the continued activity of God, and by questioning whether its self-assured purism actually embraces the loving attitude of its professed Christianity. Nonetheless, it has much to offer in its secure approach and in its resistance to modern relativism.

Obviously, Ellul has defined the idea of law on grounds which are substantially different from Berman's and which are substantially different from most other scholars. The only potential meeting ground between a Berman, who is concerned with what humans can do to improve law and religion, and an Ellul, who places the entire affair in God's hands, would be a Calvinist-like doctrine of sanctification that would allow both to agree that there are things that humans can do to improve society. This, however, does not address the ultimate question of whether those things progressively improve the human situation.

Ellul does address the purpose of human law and in doing so he makes arguments which are similar to Berman's arguments for the function of the legal dimension of religion. Ellul, of course, is ultimately negative about the results of human law saying that "[M]an is doomed to fail when he tries to create righteousness based on law, even if it is Israel."[5] The basic purpose of law, however, is to provide the framework for the spiritual event of God's speaking.[6] This purpose is very similar to Berman's purpose of law providing the context in which love may flourish. For Ellul, law should create the conditions where God's activity of mercy and forgiveness will be assisted and recognized. For Berman, law should create the conditions where love among fellow humans will flourish.

Thus, both scholars end up with very compatible purposes of human law. Their disagreement lies in where religion is found. For Ellul, God is primarily discovered in scripture and continues to act in a way consistent with scripture. For Berman, religion is a societal intuition, a perspective which can be closely correlated with Ellul's understanding of natural law.

There will most likely be aspects of natural law in all but the most totalitarian societies since there will nearly always be some spontaneous consensus of right and wrong on at least some aspects of human life. Both Berman and Ellul agree that this spontaneous natural law, or these societal intuitions, actually provide the most effective and respected law simply because law is so closely tied to religion. Thus while Ellul is certainly very Christocentric in his approach, and uses a Christocentricism which itself may be debated, it seems that there may be a meeting ground between Berman and Ellul on the following grounds:

1. That the most effective and legitimate laws exist where there is a general agreement among the people as to the values of society, values which are closely related to, if not identical to religion.

2. That useful human laws will create conditions in which love, mercy, and forgiveness will flourish.

3. That the failure to create laws influenced by religion will leave the laws ineffective, unrespected, and unenforceable except by the police power.

4. That the failure of religion to be assisted by law will make it much more difficult for love, mercy, and forgiveness to flourish.

While these common points may be used to develop an argument for the need to create a society in which these factors are present, their purposes for this book are to set the stage for the development of a broader description of religion and law that avoids institutional identifications and is useful for understanding the historical significance of religion and law in society. If this can be achieved, then some modern issues, which are almost hopelessly confused with institutional identifications with religion, may be more effectively addressed. It is time, therefore, to understand how ethics link religion and law as a way of life.

3. The Connection as a Way of Life

Sacred and Secular Ethics

Having examined the approaches of Harold Berman and Jacques Ellul, it is time to extend their analysis and develop an analysis that more broadly describes religion and its connection to law, particularly as it exists in the United States. This chapter will argue that the primary link between religion and law is the connection of religious ethics and law.

Both religious ethics and law are attempts to give order to a community, to decide what is right and wrong, to educate, and to provide an atmosphere in which people may productively live together. Both law and ethics may exist in various forms, such as custom, legislation, adjudication, or executive action, but they generally remain attempts for maintaining or adjusting the standard way of living within a community. Both reflect the values of the community that they represent.

Ethics, in fact, seem to be the very laws which Berman insists must be made part of religion. The very fact that a community exists requires an understanding of how people are to live together. Such attempts to define how people relate to other people are the very essence of ethics. Of course, once a community exists, religious notions other than ethics develop. Liturgy, ritual, and metaphysics all become critical for religion, community identification, and education. Attempting to understand inexplicable occurrences is important and attempting to understand the individual's and the community's relation to the divine is vital. These religious developments are greatly influenced by the ethical notions that

26

have already, or that are, developing. In turn, the understanding of the importance of metaphysics, liturgy, and other religious categories influences ethics, for it shows people why actions toward others are good, bad, important, or unimportant.

To illustrate this point, a simple example should suffice. If two people, who are complete strangers, meet on an abandoned pasture they immediately begin to deal with ethical concerns, even if the concern is a rudimentary agreement not to kill one another upon first sight. (For that matter, the decision to kill would itself be an ethical decision and an ethical action.) If the two are suddenly confronted with a landing spaceship which seems to be nonearthly, they are faced with trying to understand what it is that they are seeing. Their explanation, even if it is merely within each one's own head, is bound to take on some metaphysical overtones whether it be worship of the spaceship, wonderment at being visited by another being from beyond the earth, or nearly any other reaction. Regardless of their explanation, it will have some impact on defining who they are as earthly beings, why they are on earth, why they were the ones visited, and what it means to know that there are nonearthly beings, and so forth. Those metaphysical concepts will in turn make a difference to their relationship. If their reaction is fear of the unknown, they might form an alliance in order to protect themselves. If they do, they are creating an ethical atmosphere stressing the importance of their peaceful, supportive relationship. The point is that even under very rudimentary examples, people, when together, create ethical categories for action, and when the metaphysical develops (it of course may already be present), those metaphysical assumptions in turn develop the community's ethics.

Laws are society's attempt to recognize or establish ethics for a community whose membership is usually broader than that of a single religious institution or belief. Law then is not separate from ethics, nor is it separate from morality, but it is a morality and an ethic which is used by the secular community. Ethics, law, and morality are essentially the same thing, but used within a different context. By keeping law connected to secular society, morality connected to specific religious beliefs and ethics connected to both, we may eliminate some confusion.

The morality of a religious group and the law of a community may be identical if the religious body and the secular body contain the same people. For instance, in an ancient theocracy such as Israel, there was little if any difference between the laws of the nation and the morality of the religion because they were the same body. In a natural law society (using Ellul's understanding) such as pre–Great Awakening Connecticut, there would also be a very similar unity because there would have been a general consensus among the people, who nearly all belonged to the same religious body. As will be shown in Chapter 10, this results in many matters of morality being identical to laws, a situation which has caused enormous confusion among legal scholars. Thus, the religious ethics (morality) may be identical to the secular ethics (law) if there is little or no difference between the constituents of the church and the state within the community.

However, the neat connection between morality and law does not remain so neat as a community becomes religiously diverse. Once religious diversity occurs moralities will tend to differ. If this happens, the secular nation will then have to create an ethical system (i.e., a legal system which can harmoniously take into account the varying moralities). This harmonization by the legal system may not be immediate, but the secular ethics must evolve if peace is to remain. The impact of secular ethics, as well as the mere existence of pluralism, will tend to alter the morality of the religions, for each religion must contend with the knowledge that there are other ethical systems, religious and secular, which claim authority, so that each morality must in some way deal with the problems of respecting of other faiths, the roles of the church and state, and the legitimacy of their own morality.

Diversity, and the resulting conflict between moralities, may occur in several situations. It may occur within a religious body itself, as members of a congregation may develop different interpretations of what an individual or a church should do. The church must then decide which faction of its church is correct, harmonize the differing claims, or risk the fractionalization of the religious body. The situation may also arise between religious bodies where institutional jealousies, metaphysical disagreement, or personal animosity may cause Catholics to develop a different morality from Protestants, Seventh-Day Adventists from Lutherans, Mormons from Presbyterians. Finally, it can also occur between sacred and secular bodies where the interests of church and state may often differ, or where the claims of conscience require civil disobedience.

Once ethics differ, it becomes harder for consensual government to continue. Modern America, for instance, is so diverse that privatized and/or institutionalized religions regularly collide. The conflict is dangerous for it can easily escalate into intolerant hostility if a great deal of respect is not given to other moralities. It is also a brilliant opportunity to develop a newly synthesized ethic from the best parts of each morality so that harmony is preserved and a new ethic that can gain consensus is developed. This new ethic can encourage morality to provide the necessary secular framework for the toleration of diverse beliefs. Law, of course, is also prone to perpetuate the morality of the powerful and not provide for the toleration of the weak. If this is the case, civil disobedience and/or the necessity of using the state's police power will result.

Both religious ethics (morality) and secular ethics (law) are expressions of a community's beliefs. Because America is so diverse the two are even more deeply interwoven: members of each community are members of another ethical community as well. All law and morality are religious in the sense that they deal with human existence and living. Because they are so deeply interwoven in post–Enlightenment America, the best way to analyze religious and secular ethics is by looking at them as a way of life.

Looking at ethics simply as a way of deciding what actions are right and what actions are wrong is to understand ethics too narrowly. Of course ethics does involve decisions of what is right and what is wrong, but ethics is more importantly and more broadly concerned with the entire range of human activity. Contemporary ethical analysis often tends to evolve into a question of what is right and wrong, but ethics, like Berman's and Ellul's sense of the law, is an ordering process which allows love and mercy to flourish. The criteria of creating individuals and communities which do allow love and mercy to flourish means that questions other than simple right and wrong must be addressed.

While a comprehensive discussion of a methodology and philosophy of ethics is beyond the scope of this book, a brief look at two important contemporary ethicists will show the breadth and depth of ethics. (I would note that some liberty is taken in analyzing the two ethicists, Daniel Maguire and Stanley Hauerwas, because my portrayal of them may not exactly correspond to any single book which they have written. Because both men were my professors at the University of Notre Dame, I have blended their general approach, including classroom lectures, with their writings.)

Daniel Maguire describes ethics as an art/science, indicating that while logical synthesis is a part of ethics, it does not comprise all ethics. According to Maguire, moral values are what we are and that the foundation of morality is the experience of the value of persons and of affectivity. By affectivity, Maguire means that deeply centered concern and affection for other people.

Instead of concentrating on logical right and wrong distinctions, Maguire states that other sources of ethics include creative imagination, reason, principles, individual experience, authority, comedy and tragedy. Because ethics have numerous sources, ethics is much more involved than simply asking what is right and wrong, but is also involved in asking what is going on, why it is going on, how it is happening, who is involved, where it is occurring, when it is occurring and what are the viable alternatives of action. In other words, the various aspects of a situation help determine what the appropriate categories of analysis are. If one is looking at the viable alternatives, one might use creative imagination to see what can be worked out rather than looking toward authority. Ethics therefore, is concerned with all that is transpiring between and among individuals, not simply choosing between do and don't.

Although Stanley Hauerwas approaches ethics from a much different starting point than Maguire, their results, like the results of Berman and Ellul, tend to converge. Hauerwas stresses that ethics is a question of character. Ethics does not simply involve questions of decisions and action, but are moral notions, which order our lives and are the creation of our everyday habits. Habits, for Hauerwas, are those things which we are so trained to do that we do them nearly automatically. Simply because we do not go through an involved process of rationally determining whether an action is right or wrong does not mean that such an action is not an ethical act. Indeed ethics are the who we are as persons, and more importantly as communities.

For Hauerwas, ethical notions are a way of life which spring from our deeply ingrained beliefs as habits. In order to develop habits which are consistent with the teaching of Jesus Christ, we must have a Christian community which forms proper notions that allow us to develop Christian habits. The key is that the community must develop its Christian notions so that our habits are Christian. While all of this is very similar to Maguire, Hauerwas is much more deterministic and rejects the idea of a fundamental option, an option where we make a conscious decision of what is of ultimate importance. Rather, he feels that it is by the community's inculcated values that we develop ideas of right and wrong, and no option really exists which is why it is so important for the community to have the correct notions; otherwise the members of the community will not develop the essential everyday Christian habits. Still, Hauerwas and Maguire do end up in similar, although not identical, positions by stressing that ethics are who we are as persons, a meaning which indicates that far more is involved in ethics than rational decisions of right and wrong.

Ethics then are the expression of how we deal with human existence. Ethics are our priorities, our experiences, and our hopes. Ethics are attempts to order our lives so that human existence becomes meaningful. Ethics are what Berman and Ellul call law as the ordering process that allows love and mercy to flourish. Ethics are our way of life. In a very real sense, everything that we do, as habits, imagination, or other things, are ethics for they express values in a concrete context and make our values real. They also become community's and religion's expression of what is important and what is valuable and are wedded to understandings of metaphysics, pragmatism, effectiveness, and justice. Ethics emanating from metaphysical understandings become morality and ethics which emanate from human community become law.

Just as sacred ethics comprise a way of life, so do secular ethics comprise a way of life for a pluralistic community. These secular ethics are our expression of who we are, what values we hold and what we feel is important. They are our way of ordering our lives, of creating expectations, of creating conditions in which things other than mere survival may flourish.

These secular ethics are expressed in legislation as legislators attempt to enunciate principles which reflect societal values. It should also be noted that bad legislation may also exist as is the case when legislators enact laws which are not relevant to society. This circumstance also reflects upon the values of society simply because society allows such legislators to be in positions of power.

Secular ethics are also expressed in adjudication where both notions of common law, of custom, experience, precedent, and notions of application of legislation, as well as of the procedures inherent in adjudication, all reflect the important values of the society. Ethics are also expressed in custom, a notion closer to the Ellul conception of natural law where there is a generally accepted way of dealing with other people that exists powerfully, with or without legislative reinforcement. In short, secular ethics — law — expresses in a variety of forms the values which we believe are important, values which are symbols of our way of life.

Because of the diversity in America, most ethics are both secular and sacred. Ethics have aspects of both law and morality. The influence of morality upon law has always been great because so much of law is patterned after the experiences and wisdom of organized religion. They are both sacred and secular because morality and law are both addressing the problems of human existence, but from the different vantage points of religion and pluralistic society. They are also quite similar because individual religions in America must take into account the fact that there are more denominations unlike them than like them. No matter how populous the Baptists or the Roman Catholics may be, neither may claim that they alone comprise a majority of the American populace. For this reason, they must explain how they deal with other faiths, and by that concern, the religions become more like law (secular ethics), because secular ethics are always concerned with creating ethics for a pluralistic community.

Thus the important connection is this: Morality, religious

ethics, and law (secular ethics), are alike because 1) they are ethical attempts to deal with the phenomenon of human existence; 2) law has been historically dependent upon the wisdom and experience of morality; and 3) morality must become like law in order to deal with religious pluralism.

Is this connection between religion and law significant? The reader will not be astonished to learn that I think that it is so. By understanding that both religion and law are ethics, we can more properly identify what is religion and what is law, but only within a context which immediately recognizes that they are both inseparably linked. Morality and law are not similar because law is swallowed by religion (Ellul), nor are they related because they share characteristics and because they are different intuitional and ordering concepts (Berman), but because they are the same attempt to deal with human life. The difference lies in religion's moorings in transcendental concerns and/or in churches, and the law's moorings in pluralistic pragmatism.

Understanding law as secular ethics and morality as sacred ethics allows us to see that questions of whether our laws are moral are attempts to ask if metaphysical belief should be the source of secular law. If the answer is yes, society will have said that there is sufficient agreement as to the metaphysical question that a secular law may be pluralistically pragmatic. If the answer is no, society would have said that there is too much disagreement of whether or not the metaphysical belief is correct to make it a workable law in diverse America. Berman may be correct in saying that if society does not share some religious intuitions then there will not be enough legitimacy to make law effective. Ellul may be correct in saying that once general agreements of the way to live are not spontaneous, then society is on the road to decay. Beyond their insight, however, is the point that law and religion are ethical attempts to deal with human life.

A second benefit of this perspective is that by understanding ethics as a way of life, we can see the richness and depths of religious and secular ethics beyond their institutional faces. Since ethics are everyday life, the institutional component, while significant, cannot account for all that occurs in this everyday life. Hence, we can look more critically at institutions and not simply

assume that they are truly reflective of all that is occurring within
their jurisdiction. To an extent, they always will be because the
very fact that an institution continues to exist shows that the values
of society have not developed or degenerated to the stage where the
institution is no longer worth sustaining. But ethics are a more
dynamic criteria that impact and change the situation.

By looking at the way of life, the ethics, we can also see the
religion of the society. Since religious assumptions will always be
involved in stable democracies, the way of life will indicate the
values and underlying assumptions of the society. Connected with
this is the idea that the way of life perspective provides a tool for
understanding America's religious development as expressed in its
law, for the law will reflect both the moral influences of the times
and well as the secular ethical struggles of dealing with pluralism.
This analysis can also show how America's religion and law shifted
from a more institutionally based religion to one less institutionally
based. And as a final part of this connection, we can look at one
of the ways American law is produced — jurisprudence — in order
to take a look at the society's ethics, both secular and sacred. The
analysis will not be perfect, because jurisprudence is only one
aspect of law-making in America, but it is an important aspect,
and as the following pages will show, an enlightening one.

PART II
A MISSING LINK
IN AMERICAN LEGAL HISTORY

4. Moving into the Historical Context

Arguing the ethical connection of law and religion creates an interesting discussion, but the matter cannot be left on a theoretical level. Because my theory is not in vogue, it is important to flesh out some of the analysis which too narrowly limits religion and give an example of some theological analysis of jurisprudence.

Part II looks at American legal history, and attempts to determine what major scholars have meant by religion and law, and what objections there are to their approach. Prior to the actual analysis, however, it is important to understand why the historical argument has modern significance.

In the past ten years there has been a growing debate about church-state relations. The fact that Americans are discussing the relationship of these two institutions is not unusual, and the arguments are not novel. What has changed are the roles of some of the participants in the debate and the breadth of pluralistic perspective.

Among the present participants are conservative Christians, such as Protestant fundamentalists, as well as conservative Catholics. These groups have gained a great deal of popular support, support that reflects the depth and importance of the present debate. These groups protest their perception that the United States is steadily moving away from the Judeo-Christian values upon which the country was founded. These groups insist that the United States, to be moral, must incorporate the substantive doctrines which have sustained it throughout the past two hundred

37

years. In short, these groups believe that America was founded on
Judeo-Christian values, and insist upon the maintenance of those
values.

On the other side of the debate is a group that could be called
the moderate traditionalists. This group is frightened by the calls
of the Judeo-Christian conservatives. Their argument is the very
American notion that every person should be allowed to worship
freely as he or she chooses without coercion or fear of reprisal from
other religious groups. Religion, it is thought, is a private matter,
and while there is nothing "wrong" with the conservative beliefs of
their opponents, there is something wrong with the imposition of
conservative beliefs on the country in the form of law. The
moderate traditionalists base their argument on the American
history of tolerating a religiously pluralistic nation.

What has brought this debate to its present temperature (and
the temperature is very likely to continue its rise) is the question
of whether religious groups should band together to form political
associations with power sufficient to enact laws to their liking. For
decades religious groups have watched an America governed by
interest groups. Since World War II automobile manufacturers,
high technology concerns, blacks, dairy farmers, women, gun
owners and homosexuals have created politically powerful
organizations with the ability to influence people in government.
Conservative religious people have watched such groups shape
some laws which are directly contrary to their sacred beliefs. Using
interest-group politics, these conservative religious groups have
banded together to also influence people in government to enact
laws favorable to their conservative interests. These conservatives
feel that they are restoring Judeo-Christian laws by methods ap-
proved by American society and its constitutions.

The moderate traditionalists, however, claim that there is
something special about religion. Although few have raised the
point quite so baldly, the crux of the sentiment is that religion is
far too dangerous and too life-centering to allow it to be used in
the normal interest group manner. Religion, as a private affair, is
not a subject which can be imposed upon other people by
government.

Both groups fail to realize the conceptual weakness of the

doctrine of the separation of church and state. This weakness is perpetuated by historians. Americans fail to realize that there is a major difference between religion and church and also a difference between state and politics (including law). Religion, including Judeo-Christian religion, is much broader and much deeper than the notion of the institutional church. Politics and law are much deeper than the institutional state. The moderate traditionalists and the conservatives are essentially arguing over which religion will govern America. The conservatives are correct in recognizing the moderate traditionalists' beliefs as a religion dominating American society; the moderate traditionalists are correct in questioning whether the values of the conservatives encompass all the historical values of America.

This section proposes to show how contemporary legal historians, primarily writing from an economic perspective, have perhaps unintentionally misled Americans by ignoring the religious component of the country. This failure has blurred our perception of the content of religion, and has made it difficult to understand the true argument in contemporary America. The religious component has always been present, but the language by which it has been expressed has been as fluid as the nation itself.

Historically, Americans wanted to be free of an established church and the opportunity to worship freely was relished by American Puritans and Quakers settling the country. As the colonies matured, they became more religiously diverse, particularly after the shattering of religious unity caused by the Great Awakening of 1740. Thereafter, freedom from an established church gained other support. For many, the presence of a state-sponsored church was an unpleasant reminder of England. It was also an unwelcomed, even obnoxious burden financially because of the requirement to pay taxes to support the state's church. For others, a general fear of both episcopacy and papacy was reason enough to oppose any form of church-state alliance. In the federal constitution, and gradually in the state constitutions, churches were disestablished.

The content of American religion was generally Protestant, and more specifically Calvinist (most of the denominations in America before the Civil War were). Of course, Presbyterian and

Congregational denominations were theologically tied to Calvinism, and because of the effects of the Great Awakening, Methodist, Episcopal, and Baptist denominations were also so. These latter Calvinist faiths achieved the freedom of worship and the national toleration of denominationalism with the disestablishment of churches in the federal and state constitutions. Their victory, however, was not easy, as the established churches thought that disestablishment would be tantamount to debauchery, and restricted complete freedom of worship.

The new idea that the church and the state were divided by a wall of separation did not render America a-religious. Throughout its history, America remained religious, and did so quite consciously. In fact, as Catherine Albanese has insightfully described, America continued to practice the Protestant Code. According to Albanese, there are six elements of the code:

> 1. The notions of religious liberty for all people and the democratic equality of all people.
> 2. The separation of the institutions of church and state.
> 3. The notions of denominationalism instead of unitary religion and voluntarism instead of forced denominational affiliation.
> 4. The trait of church activism so that the members of the faith would get the message of their denomination to other citizens.
> 5. The notions of reductionism and anti-intellectualism which resulted in ethical and political questions framed in either/or terminology with the alternatives defined in good against evil phraseologies in as simple words as possible.
> 6. Moralism so that morality was the key to Christian life, an idea that defined national policies and struggles, such as seeing the Civil War as a moralistic crusade (on both sides).[1]

By about 1830, America had successfully become a religiously pluralistic nation within the bounds of Calvinism. The Protestant Code was firmly established as the country's religion and the vast majority of denominations were Calvinist. The slow acceptance of religious groups did not remain solely within Protestant denominations. New non–Protestant groups came to America and fought the same battles for religious freedom as the non–Puritan Protestants fought. For example, the American Catholic population swelled with the periodic flood of immigration, and the

Catholics were not always free from persecution. Their struggle continued even into the last generation when the faith and allegiance of John F. Kennedy were issues in the 1960 presidential campaign. However, two things happened: first, the Jewish and the Catholic faiths became "Americanized" and thereby incorporated the Protestant Code into their American faith; and second, the toleration of American religious pluralism gradually expanded to include acceptance of some non–Protestant traditions.

The influence of the Protestant Code was felt even among non–Calvinists in several ways. One way was by civil religion. America inherited and built upon the Puritan notions of religion and identified the United States as an actor in God's plan of salvation.

> Civil religion grew and changed throughout American history, and its presence was particularly visible in millenial fervor during wartime. Yet its essentials came from the seventeenth and eighteenth centuries. By the time George Washington took his oath of office as first president of the United States, the fundamentals of the civil religion were in place. They had arisen out of New England Puritanism, but especially out of the fusion of Puritanism with the engagement of Americans in Revolutionary War. In this setting, the Puritan past was re-interpreted, linked more strongly to the Enlightenment (it had already been so linked), and joined finally to the legend that Americans were creating by their own deeds in the war-deeds that were widely understood as the beginning of a millennial era.[2]

There is little doubt that Americans viewed themselves as a new Israel, a new chosen people, and Protestants, Jews, and Catholics could relate to, believe in, and live with that religious metaphor.

Calvinist beliefs also influenced the rest of the country through the education system. One of the great achievements of Puritan New England was the establishment of an effective school system. When other colonies instituted their own educational systems, they naturally looked to the Puritan example.[3] The New England primers, which were widely used, taught work ethic values, and espoused a Calvinist world-view. Hence, the education of American children was couched in Calvinist terms, a process whose influence cannot be underestimated.

What does this brief sketch mean for the modern debates of religion and politics? The modern struggle is essentially a repetition of earlier struggles with a slightly different language. American religious diversity has expanded beyond the boundaries of Judeo-Christian faith, an expansion which pits the concrete values of traditional Judeo-Christian faith against the value of privatization and tolerance of individual religion. Concrete Judeo-Christian values, such as the preservation of human life, run headlong into the insistence that an abortion is a matter of individual choice. The debate has been dormant because there was little conflict between the idea of toleration of religious diversity and laws which were essentially from the Judeo-Christian tradition. The debate over separation of church and state was not as virulent because there were fewer instances of non–Judeo-Christian policy implementations. The fact that there are such policy questions now brings forth the old arguments of separating religion from law. In fact, the argument is not about separating religion from law, but is about the content of the religion from which law emanates. Both toleration of religious pluralism and concrete religious ethics are religious values. The contemporary question is whether toleration of American diversity will expand to include the values of the moderate traditionalists or whether the toleration will remain within the bounds of Judeo-Christian ethics.

To use the terminology of the first section, contemporary America is struggling between the content of sacred and secular ethics. Both the religions of conservatives and moderate traditionalists are attempting to enforce their sacred ethics (morality), upon all of society through secular ethics (law). Because morality is thereby directly challenged, conflict becomes inevitable. The conflict is indicative of a lack of societal consensus on at least some issues, and if the conflict is not harmoniously resolved, law will exist without Ellul's natural law spontaneity and without Berman's societal intuitions. This result would encourage, and has encouraged, the loss of respect for at least some law. To resolve the conflict, all must closely examine their morality to see whether the morality of each ultimately requires civil disobedience or whether morality can allow for conscientious compromise. A first step toward such an examination is to study history.

While there are many reasons for the contemporary confusion in religion and law, a primary villain is the analysis that has been used by contemporary legal historians. In sketching the development of American jurisprudence, they have understood religion almost exclusively in its manifestation as an institutional church, an analysis which incorrectly understands religion, particularly in the United States. It identifies being religious as being churchly and being economic or secular as being modern and a-religious.

Historians have tended to analyze American legal history in a two-step analysis. The common breaking point between the two steps is a period nearly coinciding with the American Revolution. The first period was American colonial law. In this prerevolutionary time, law was heavily influenced by religious values and institutions. During this time there was a static society which consciously understood itself to be a religious society. The second step, however, takes into account the industrial revolution and the Enlightenment. This postrevolutionary period was and is governed by the laws of eonomics. This theory incorrectly implies two things: that religion is synonymous with a pre–industrial revolution mentality which is an old-fashioned, Puritan concern for rules and regulations, and that religion means church domination of society, a domination which fails to be "modern."

Such a theory is gravely inaccurate. So much of this theory is obviously true, however, that it normally stands unchallenged. One cannot argue that the dynamic economic forces unleashed by the industrial revolution had an enormous impact on the law of society. Nor can one argue with the fact that there was something different about America after disestablishment. The argument, however, does not take into account that the growing power of the mercantile class began long before the American Revolution and had an impact on American law before the Revolution, nor does it take into account the conscious American self-identification as a religious people in a religious nation. Specifically, the theory of the economic historians does not account for the Puritan notion that the pursuit of wealth was part of a religious life. Thus, the Puritan ideology, which has been the American ideology, smoothly blended the pursuit of economic wealth and power with pietistic living both before and after the American Revolution.

It is beyond the scope of this section to develop a philosophical analysis of the interaction of economics and spirituality, but this section does attempt to analyze the work of some economic historians. This analysis will concentrate on the work of the legal historians such as William Nelson, Willard Hurst, Lawrence Friedman, and Morton Horwitz. In analyzing these historians, the work of Richard Posner will also be briefly noted in order to sketch the consequences of the economic approach to law. There also will be a very brief sketch of an alternative to the economic approach proposed by Stephen Presser. By making this analysis, the section will show that while the economic approach is a legitimate understanding of American law, it is an understanding which far too narrowly limits the richness and depth of American history.

5. The Theory of the Economic Historians

William Nelson and
"Americanization of the Common Law" (1975)

William Nelson, an early contemporary legal historian, used the economic analysis of legal history. Nelson made an exhaustive study of the law of Massachusetts and reached the conclusion that early Massachusetts society was bound together by an "ethical unity," but was later governed by a legal system deeply influenced, if not manipulated, by strong economic interests.

The young colony was a static rural community which had scant interest in economic growth or speculation. It was bound together by an ethical unity enforced as custom, which was primarily interested in fairness of the law, and the jury was the primary tool used to resolve disputes or impose sanctions. The Congregational Church, the church of the Puritans, was the established church, and the primary goal of this churchly society was to preserve the status quo with its inherent claims of God's truth and justice.[1]

By 1830, the complexion of Massachusetts society had radically changed. According to Nelson, the most important development was the disestablishment of the church:

> ... disestablishment marked the final end of the era in which men
> thought it proper for government and related institutions to impose
> a common set of ethical values on individuals in the community who
> did not voluntarily share them.[2]

In the manner typical of the economic historians, Nelson vastly overestimates the role of the institutional church in the life of religion. Although there was no longer an institutional religious body supported by the state, there remained the established religion of the Protestant Code as well as the Christian concepts of the growth of the law, the individual's right to contract and own property, and the idea of government by the consent of the governed. Moreover, religious people shared the notions that America was a chosen nation and that Americans were chosen people. While institutions are as important in American society as in any other society, they do not entirely account for the motivating beliefs of society, the people who create institutions, and the people who operate them. Since Nelson's approach is representative of the other historians, it is worth taking some time to explore exactly what he means when he categorizes prerevolutionary America as a Christian state.

Nelson explicitly deals with the "Law of a Christian and Civil State" in Massachusetts, but unfortunately limits this concept to criminal punishments for violations of religious laws and fails to include the economic nature of the Christian state. Most of these crimes were crimes against God and religion, such as fornication, fraud, indecency and usury. In punishing the violators of God's law, Nelson says that the violators were not viewed as outcasts, but simply as fellow sinners who had sinned.[3] These characteristics, Nelson believes, are evidence of and descriptive of the "Christian State."

Nelson's analysis, however, too narrowly articulates the religious nature of colonial Massachusetts. There can be no doubt that Massachusetts Puritans were Calvinistically aware of themselves as being sinners in the eyes of God; but it is also important to remember that the degree of punishment inflicted upon a violator, as well as the attitude that society held toward the violator, were also dependent upon the religious fervor of the time. Although it has perhaps been an overblown affair, the Salem witchcraft trials were not simply punishments of fellow sinners who had sinned, but punishment of evil-doers. Much of the Puritan fervor of the witchcraft era diminished through the eighteenth century. In fact, one of the causes of the Great Awakening of

1740 was undoubtedly a reaction to the decreased piety of the Puritans. In short, Nelson may be correct in noting that at certain times, and in some infractions, a violator was simply a fellow sinner who had sinned, but the attitude toward violators varied with the religious times.

Ironically, Nelson may have understated the religious character of the Massachusetts Christian state. While the role of the strictly Puritan church was diminished after the Great Awakening, the role of religion was not. Nelson states that by 1760, juries were applying puritanical traditions even though Puritans were no longer as influential.[4] The reason for the juries applying puritanical traditions was that although Massachusetts was initially confronting religious diversity, it was diversity among Calvinist denominations who shared the basic traditions and theologies of Puritans. Massachusetts was not becoming less of a Christian state, its Christianity was simply being stretched so that puritanical traditions were accepted and practiced by Puritans and non-Puritans as part of a national adherence to the new, established religion of the Protestant Code. The morality of the Puritans was stretched by contact with non-Puritans, but the secular ethic was so similar in terms of the Protestant Code, that there was little sustained conflict between law and religion.

Another fundamental characteristic of colonial legal society was the restraint of arbitrary power. As part of the philosophy which created the federal system of checks and balances, the colonists sought to curtail the power of all groups, persons, or institutions. For instance, requiring a judge to follow precedent prevented him from altering or creating law to suit his own purposes. Another major limitation on judicial power was the jury, since in colonial America the jury had the authority to decide questions of both law and fact. Even though the judge did not have the authority to create new law, the jury did. In fact, if a judge informed the jury of the applicable law, the colonial jury had the freedom to simply ignore the judge and do whatever it pleased.[5]

The role of the jury should not be overestimated, however, as there were restraints placed upon it also. The developing law of evidence kept testimony away from the jury. Some types of evidence, such as hearsay, were deemed to be unreliable, and while the citizens trusted the jury more than they trusted judges, the fact remains that even the jury was denied absolute power in American society.

The notion of restraint of arbitrary power also applied to other organs of the government. In colonial Massachusetts the legislature was the primary governing body. More specifically, the legislature was known as the General Court, which was a unitary governing body possessing legislative, judicial and executive functions. Nelson emphasizes that the General Court was actually fairly weak, the executive aspect even weaker, with the primary power being the town meeting.[6]

The restraint of arbitrary power and the strength of the town meeting are tied to the notion of the democratic equality of people, which is part of the Protestant Code. To protect the equality of people, the society developed procedures that, Nelson discovers, prevent excessive personal or institutional power. It is important, however, to remember that democratic equality was not colonially conceived to be equality of all persons, but equality within a certain group, namely white, propertied males. Democratic equality, like religious toleration, was a concept developed within certain experiential frameworks, but which were concepts that could and did expand to apply to more people than had been initially intended. Thus, the colonial governmental system was directly part of the Protestant Code, which was societally malleable, and was appealing to and protective of most moralities of the times, so that religion and law harmoniously embraced limitations on arbitrary power. Such limitations may prevent one's personal morality from dominating, and since the bottom-line law was acceptable, conflict was small.

Nelson's third characterization of Massachusetts society was that there were strong rules of unity and stability as well as a sense of hierarchy in Massachusetts society, a hierarchy manifested, for instance, in the tradition of apprenticeship.[7] Thus, there was a certain agreement that some people were better than others, that some people, by nature, performed different functions than others, and that some people possessed rights to the exclusion of others (such as the right to vote, held by propertied, white males). The function of law was to perpetuate the hierarchical system that existed. Fairness and stability were integral parts in this system of accepted inequalities. Therefore, the law had a "fair" notion of contracts so that speculative contracts and one-sided contracts would not be enforced, and all people would have some basic societal protection.[8] But colonial America and colonial law did not remain stationary. The change was fueled by the growing economic demands of the country. In short, according to Nelson, economic growth caused the end of the religious domination of society. This is a vast overstatement, indeed it is an incorrect statement of what occurred in American society, but since it is a theory that clearly dominates American legal history, it is important to examine Nelson's contribution to this theory.

Nelson is absolutely correct in noting the major demographic change of America between 1780 and 1830. During this time, the country changed from an agrarian society to an industrialized market society. Nelson argues that this demographic change led to an increasingly materialistic and commercial view of humanity.[9] That is also probably true, but it is important to remember that the religion in colonial times and in these newly industrial times was perfectly suited to accept both the rural agrarian market and the industrial market.

One of the strengths of Calvinist belief is its idea that the individual can serve God vocationally. This means that a person can be the loyal, faithful servant of God in a job other than the clergy. Further, Calvinist followers thought that success in one's occupation was a sign of God's favor. In fact, to be successful in business was itself a sign of faithfulness. When the industrial revolution struck, a conflicting choice between being economically successful against being religious did not exist. The members of the Presbyterian, Congregational, and Episcopal faiths were far more urban than their Methodist and Baptist counterparts, but all these strong denominations were Calvinist, and each could fill a role in the industrial revolution. A Calvinist denomination existed for both the rural and urban parts of society, and overlaying the entire society was the established religion of the Protestant Code. In short, America remained a Calvinist country even after the explosion of the industrial revolution.

Did America change from being religious to being materialistic, and did the extent to which religious values were enforced by others change during this period, as Nelson claims?[10] It is certainly probable that Americans became more materialistic with the advent of the market economy, but as already stressed, that change was a change within religious terminology. Americans did not become a-religious with the presence of the market economy; rather, American Calvinist theology found new factual applications for its world-view. Once this is understood, it becomes obvious that religious values were still very much being imposed on people by others, but these new religious values were unlike the strictly "fair" values of colonial religion.

Nelson continues his analysis by noting various instances in which the old ideas of religious fairness were replaced by the new ideas of aggressive, competitive economics. For instance, he says that the exaltation of private property and the idea of freedom of contract undermined the ethical unity and stability of colonial law.[11]

However, what actually was happening was an increasingly positive view of the significance of the individual, a view that is quite Protestant. It is true that the law focused on allowing the individual to have much more freedom, but again, that did not eliminate the religious character of the law, but rather, infused it with the new religious terminology of Christian responsibility, opportunities for doing good works, and the ability to reject law which contradicted God's law.

This analysis of William Nelson's work is generally applicable for all of the economic historians. They share the concept of a religious colonial era being supplanted by an economic, industrial era. Different historians will use different means to express and illustrate their theory, so it is important to consider some of their other works.

Before proceeding to the more radical economists such as Morton Horwitz and Richard Posner, it is time to look at the more traditional historians who have been labeled the "Wisconsin School": Lawrence Friedman and J. Willard Hurst.[12]

Lawrence Friedman and
"A History of American Law" (1973)

Lawrence Friedman's book brought a new focus to the study of American legal history. *A History of American Law* was the first truly comprehensive treatment of American legal history. Friedman set the initial standard for American legal history as Nelson did for the legal history confined to a single state. Although necessarily more comprehensive than Nelson's study, the themes of the two scholars are certainly not antipodal.

For Friedman, law is a mirror of society and a study of social development.[13] Thus the priorities and values of a given society will be reflected in the law that is created. The law is eternally new, because each society selects those aspects of previous law that are useful and practical, rejects what is no longer practical, and creates new forms that are required. In Friedman's theory, colonial legal development was a time of simplification of the law so that it would be accessible to common people. From the Revolutionary War to the death of Chancellor Kent in 1847, Americans curtailed arbitrary power and instrumentally used law and government for economic development. Although Friedman uses a slightly different slant than Nelson, he does share the idea that economics supplanted religion.

Central to Friedman's theory is his understanding of the subject matter of the colonial courts. He says that the single-bodied colonial government delegated authority to courts to resolve disputes, with the key forum being the county court.[14] However, decentralization of judicial authority did not follow the English pattern. Friedman notes that, unlike England, America had no ecclesiastical courts.[15] Thus probate and family law matters that would have been presented to English ecclesiastical courts were instead presented to the regular American court system. There are good reasons for this that Friedman does not note.

As Everett Goodwin has brilliantly illustrated in Connecticut jurisprudence, one of the direct influences of Calvinism was the adoption of a magesterial form of government.[16] This was a form of government advocated by Calvin based on the Hebrew system of government found in the biblical book of Judges. The magistrate, an elected official, was to rule according to the will of God, and the people were to elect magistrates who would enact the will of God. There was no disjunction between secular and sacred matters. Variations of this Calvinist form of government were seen in nearly every other colonial government, and reveal that American colonial government, including its court system, was specifically founded upon Calvinist origins. The elimination of ecclesiastical courts in America was made precisely because the entire society was religious, but in a language unlike England's. The evolution to a more sophisticated governmental structure thus took place within an accepted religious conception of jurisprudence as the applied will of God. That will of God was the product of everyday problems, including commercial disputes.

He stresses that colonial law moved toward the simplification of courtroom procedure. Previously, common law pleading was exceptionally intricate and simplification was an effort to make law understandable to society and to reduce the need for excessive lawyerly intervention. He specifically ties this simplification to the reforming zeal of the Puritans. He also correctly notes that merchants and landowners gained in governmental influence, and wanted a rational and efficient system of jurisprudence. However, he misses the fact that the zeal of the Puritans and the interests of the economically progressive were part of the same spirit.[17]

Friedman does not explicitly stress the essentially religious character of American colonial government, though he does definitely recognize it. As he describes postrevolutionary America, Friedman focuses on the relation between the people and the state to the exclusion of religion. He too identifies religion and state in narrow, institutional manifestations without fully understanding the continuing religious nature of postrevolutionary America.

Friedman claims that the state was not, as often assumed, strictly in a laissez-faire role, but was actively involved in the development of American society. The government chartered corporations, particularly transportation companies such as canal, bridge, road, and railroad builders. This state involvement was supported by the American people:

> . . . most Americans no doubt felt that the state should encourage development, though perhaps they also felt that the state, like the Lord, helped those who helped themselves. [18]

It would be a mistake to use Friedman's religious analogy to show that the people viewed the government as a sort of deity. However, it is instructive to realize that the Puritan religious government also found the need to use the law instrumentally as a teacher. Tapping Reeve, a Connecticut Supreme Court justice, once stressed the importance of using the Bible to understand the laws of the state, and for the state to educate children in the ways of the Lord. [19] Every government has an instrumental aspect and uses law as a tool to achieve the ends that it desires. Whereas colonial America may have tied that instrumentality to specific religious doctrines, the postrevolutionary instrumentality also had a religious purpose, namely supporting the goodness of accumulating wealth, a goodness sanctioned by the doctrines of Calvinist America and by the established religion of the Protestant code.

One of the most significant developments in American legal history was the use of reported cases and legal treatises. As Grant Gilmore said, there cannot be a legal system until case reports are regularly published. [20] Friedman explains that in colonial times, there were no published reports of cases, no legal journals, and only Blackstone's *Commentaries* as a treatise. In colonial America, judges applied the common law, but the common law was a murky body of precedent. The age of publishing reports coincided with the explosion of the Enlightenment, so judges in the postrevolutionary period had to confront the fact that their opinions were to be reported and circulated among the other states, and that the intellectual climate demanded some type of logical rationality in these opinions. Previously, it was not difficult to overlook contradiction in rules when judges did not have to publicly reconcile them. Much of the disregard for precedent among postrevolutionary American judges can be explained not simply in terms of economic development, but in the direct confrontation of judges with precedential theories of law which were not necessarily harmonious with other theories. The importance of the written law in

American history cannot be overestimated. Friedman is correct in noting its importance, for it was the rational exposition of legal principles applied to society that formed the texts of American jurisprudential faith.

Friedman argues that in the latter part of the nineteenth century, the interests of commercial business were favored, and like Nelson, notes the victory over religion. In tort law, absolute liability (primarily of railroads) was rejected in favor of an ambiguous "reasonable man" standard which generally used an economic balancing test favoring enterprise. The rights of victims were further hampered by doctrines such as assumption of risk, contributory negligence, and the fellow-servant rule. Some of these limitations were offset by the last clear chance doctrine (when contributory negligence of the plaintiff will not bar his action if the defendant had a clear chance of avoiding inflicting injury had he exercised due care), and *res ipsa loquitor* (when mere proof that an accident took place is sufficient under the circumstances to warrant on inference that it was caused by the defendant's negligence, unless otherwise explained), but generally, the victim did not have as many legal tools to use as did the enterprises perpetrating the injury.[21]

In contract law, the courts generally enforced what the parties had agreed to instead of forcing a "fair" notion of exchange upon the transaction. However, just as *res ipsa loquitor* and the last clear chance doctrine had some mitigating effect on the weapons of business, the courts also slowly began to imply warranties to sales of merchandise. Friedman points out that these warranties were not the twentieth century type seeking to protect the consumer, but primarily were warranties of sales of merchandise from one business to another. Still, there is little question that the nineteenth century courts were primarily interested in enforcing a "will theory" of contracts, and primarily protected developing business at the expense of the victims injured in its development.[22]

Friedman incorrectly separates these developments from religious ideas of law. He continues the mistaken notion that economic interests and the pursuit of wealth were a-religious in America when in fact they were very much part of the same ideology. He further breaks economics from religion in his argument that in the nineteenth century there was a victory over religion. The evidence Friedman uses for this concerns divorce and marriage laws, usury laws, and the temperance movement.

Friedman states that "[I]n the law of marriage and divorce, religion, sentiment and morals influenced the law, along with economic and business motives." By this, Friedman apparently means that religious beliefs discouraging divorce blended with economic forces to produce a law of divorce. He further states that the usury laws were not based in ideology, but in economic interest, since where money was scarce, the rates were legally higher than where money was plentiful. Finally, he states that the temperance movement was a battle over whose norms were dominant, old-line middle class, rural Protestant, or immigrant, urban Catholic.[23]

Friedman is very close to realizing the point of this section. He is critical of the looseness of the usury rates, but that looseness is itself indicative of the flexibility of religious norms. No ethic, sacred or secular, exists simply in a static form, but evolves as it is challenged and modified by encounters with other faiths. Friedman unfortunately insists on viewing religion as a system of ironclad rules. There is a strong tradition in America for viewing religion in this same ironclad, rule-oriented, institutional way, but religion is more broadly a way of life and an experience rather than institutional allegiance, so that changes do occur in religion, changes which do not destroy religion, but which often change its character. It would be a mistake to insist that religion, which must deal with the problems of believers, must remain static when problems and societies change. Religion grows, changes, and develops according to the experiences of its communal existence.

Friedman's examples differ from Nelson's, and for the most part, he is more subtle in articulating a change from religion to economics. His underlying separation of the industrial revolution from religion, however, is nearly identical to Nelson's. Both insist upon using an institutional caricature of religion instead of understanding religion's breadth and flexibility, particularly in the existence of Calvinism in America.

J. Willard Hurst and
"Law and the Conditions of Freedom" (1956)

More than any of the economic historians, J. Willard Hurst explicitly articulates the nature of humanity in describing his legal theory. Any conception of humanity is a vital religious question; indeed, many would argue that anthropology is the essence of religion. Not only do atheists such as Feuerbach, Freud, and Marx concentrate on the anthropology in criticizing religion, but prominent Christian theologians such as Karl Rahner begin their theology by attempting to understand humanity.

Hurst believes that the lines of public policy in the nineteenth century revolved around the idea that human nature was creative. During this time, the meaning of life depended on possessing a wide range of options and choices. The function of the law was therefore to protect and promote individual creative energy, and the legal order was to use resources to shape the environment to give men more liberty.[24] Immediately one can see that Hurst comes much closer to grasping the complexity of the societal milieu that created an instrumental law that encouraged the development of the industrial revolution. Hurst accurately perceives that the underlying motivations of this law are grounded in the conception of humanity, conceptions that consciously use religious language.

However, Hurst does not extend this concept to fully appreciate the religious nature of the times. Most of his analysis is in terms of the economic development of society and the economic predispositions of the law. He feels that economics was in fact the motivating force behind these legal developments. For instance, the notions of freedom of contract and the marketability of real property instead of the static theory of contract and primogeniture were both based on the economic needs of an expanding society. The Dartmouth College case showed a mid-century preference for growth instead of security. This burst of economic growth, which Hurst dubs the "release of energy" was primarily an economic activity.[25]

So where does that leave the religious nature of the law? What happens to the anthropological anchors which seemed so promising? Unfortunately, Hurst has also fallen to the notions of religion in institutional terms, or for him, more specifically in philosophical terms. Hurst says that Americans were people who were going places in a hurry and who had no time to philosophize. Politics and humanitarianism were not as important to the nineteenth century human as was making a successful living.[26] But again, making religion into a tightly patterned activity that only has to do with good deeds, metaphysics, and institutional allegiances robs the reality of the notion that religion is a way of life.

Religion is an orientation of being that gives meaning and focus to a person's existence. This is admittedly a broad definition of religion; it is vulnerable to the criticism that if religion is a way of life, then everyone has a religion.[27] Actually, this is correct. Each person does have a religion, a way of orienting one's life. To use religion in this sense does not relativize religion into murky meaninglessness; it means that each person has a way of orienting life, but the legitimacy of such an orientation remains open to critical evaluation.

In America, however, we do not have to reach so far to make nineteenth century law religious. Nineteenth century law was not religious simply because everyone had a religion, but because nineteenth century Calvinism provided a theological justification for the needs of the industrial revolution. Calvinism was modified by the Enlightenment and Arminianism, both of which gave much more emphasis to the creative ability of the individual. Wedded with that individualism was the idea of serving God vocationally, with wealth as a sign of a goodly life. The result was a theology that encouraged, supported, and justified the economic explosion of the industrial revolution in nineteenth century America.

In short, Hurst comes close to realizing the religious nature of law by his focus on anthropology, but he then fails to continue his insight to understand that anthropology had a basis in the nineteenth century theology of Calvinism. That failure forces him to miss the linkage between economic and religious America.

Other historians have performed a vitally important role in the contemporary inauguration of the study of legal history and have understandably done so in the terminology of our times, namely that of sensitivity to economic factors. The criticism of this section is not that economic forces did not grow powerful, for it is absolutely true that the effects of the industrial revolution were deeply felt in American jurisprudence. Rather, it is that the development of American law was nurtured, sustained, and encouraged by the developing religious notions, notions that cannot be contained in simple institutional terminology. The danger of the economic historians is that they assume that religion was vanquished with the industrial revolution. Those who agree with that theory are then surprised when suddenly there are potent religious confrontations as are in our society today. The fact is that the country continued to be religious, but since the religion was so deeply harmonious with the development of our economic society, it was taken for granted and ignored. It has reared its head on the occasions when different aspects of that religion suddenly clash as they did in the early nineteenth century common law. Because secular ethics were supported by a general consensus of Calvinism, there was little "morality argument" on social, economic, or military policy. When society was first experiencing the effects of pluralism, even within Calvinism, the volatility of the debate rose, just as it has in contemporary America.

The implications of following a strictly economic approach to the law are dangerous and powerful. Two scholars who have followed this approach are Morton Horwitz and Richard Posner. Horwitz develops the approach in historical terms, while Posner actually develops a theory of analyzing the law in philosophical terms. It is important to grasp the implications of the economic approach, so a short analysis of each is in order.

Morton Horwitz and
"The Transformation of American Law" (1977)

When Morton Horwitz published his Bancroft Prize–winning book, he touched off a controversy that has yet to subside. A plethora of articles have been written about the book, many favorable and some simply scathing. He has been criticized on a great many fronts both substantively and methodologically, yet there remains a great appeal in his work. Part of the appeal is the fact that Horwitz was able to analyze the development of law in categorical terms which oversimplify, but which also reveal a general truth.

The basic Horwitz thesis is that in the eighteenth century there was a static society that had notions of fairness used to guide the law. The common law was a kind of natural law in which permanency and stability were revered and in which precedent was strictly followed. However, because of the murkiness of the common law, there was also a degree of unpredictability, particularly for the commercial classes whose economic interests demanded some sense of predictability. In the last fifteen years of the eighteenth century, judges started reasoning about the social consequences of the law. Conflicts were noted in the law, and the notion of a permanent natural law foundation of the common law disintegrated to a view of the foundation of the common law being consensus among the people. Once this notion of consensual custom was admitted, it was noted that individuals were the ones creating the consensus. Thus, the notions of the power of individuals creating law was established. In the eighteenth century, the wills were consensual and static, but in the nineteenth century, individual wills diverged, so courts allowed a "will theory" to be established in which the courts would enforce whatever the individual wills had agreed upon in a contract, whether it was fair or not.[28]

Coincident to this intellectual development was the rise of the merchant class. The powerful merchant class took control of the legal system so that the "will theory" predominated which allowed entrepreneurs the freedom to deal any way they saw fit. After the merchant class had made their gains, they retrenched and manipulated the courts into a legal formalism which protected the interests of the wealthy, and then prevented excessive speculation.[29]

Horwitz's theory makes great dramatic reading, and may even be true. The difficulty is that he ascribes an enormous amount of conscious planning over an extended period of time to a commercial group which was incredibly competitive. Horwitz's theory requires the belief of merchants acting in concert to control the law while slitting each other's throats. Although there is evidence that the Horwitz theory does not stand, one can argue that the basic theory is not disproven and that the development of law did favor enterprise and did slow down to protect the gains of enterprise near the time of the Civil War.[30]

So what's wrong, from a religious perspective, with Horwitz? Horwitz seems to ignore, even more than other economic historians, the role religion has played in the development of law. Other than vaguely describing colonial law as a kind of "natural law," a term that is fraught with centuries of difficulties, he does not even consider the impact of religion either before or after the transformation. To say that there was an "equitable notion of con- tract" based on "fairness" says nothing about the basis of criminal law, of "laws against God and religion," of the theological nature of static society in the form of magesterial government, or of the emotional desire of freedom of religious worship before the transformation; nor does it say anything about the change in the attitude of the individual within humanity, the metaphysical understanding of the "release of energy," the religious sense of manifest destiny, or the Calvinist encouragement of wealth in serving God. Horwitz's focus is so narrow, that the depth and com- plexity of American legal history is lost. Few individuals, if any, and fewer societies, if any, can be categorized into a single concep- tual story. Horwitz, however, attempts to do this by his focus on the transformation of American law resulting from the economic surge of power of the mercantile class.

Before proceeding to Richard Posner, it is fair to pose the same objection to his section as is posed to Horwitz: namely, that religion is far too narrow of a focus to understand jurisprudence, just as Horwitz's economic analysis is too narrow. The answer is a qualified "no," and fairly enough, the Horwitz focus could con- ceivably be broad enough if one uses some of Posner's approaches which will be described soon.

As stated previously, the problem with analyzing jurispru- dence in religious terms is that most people immediately associate religion with the institutional church or a set of ironclad rules. If religion is limited in this manner, it most assuredly is not capable of grasping the breadth of law. If, however, religion is understood as a way of life, as an orientation of individuals and of society, then religion allows for a spectrum of analysis which includes nontraditionally religious ideas such as economics, politics, and law while maintaining one of religion's strengths: sensitivity to the motivating spiritual and philosophical justifications and experiences of society. In America, religion encompassed all. It was neither the religion of institutions, for America has had such a potpourri of denominations that no institution has dominated, nor the ironclad rules, for no power has been present to enforce ironclad religious commands. But America did develop an ideology of Albanese's Protestant Code which perpetuated Calvinist understandings of society, of humanity, and of goodness. This ideology was not stagnant, but developed so that the individual gained much more importance, so that the country became not only Calvinist, but Judeo-Christian, and perhaps now, practices some sort of general humanitarianism. Using religion in this sense, it is not only a useful tool, but is perhaps the only tool which can capture the richness and depth of the American jurisprudential experience.

Richard Posner and "Economic Analysis of Law" (1972)

By this time the reader will anticipate that I will not be favorable toward a scholar who analyzes law solely in economic terms. And while the reader will be correct, I would like to begin with a more favorable note, one which can allow the economic analysis of the law if one uses one of Posner's concepts.

Posner objects to the notion that economics is about money; instead, he says that economics is about resources.[31] Thus, if economics is a science used to show how resources can best be used to increase human satisfaction, then we can understand resources in a much deeper sense than merely being opportunity costs.

Therefore, we need to view all valuable resources, such as traditions, family, spiritual experience, emotional feelings, as well as
production of materials, profit, and opportunity costs in order to
gain a perspective of American law. If this approach is truly followed, economic analysis of the law could grasp the value of the
underlying motivations which undergird law and society and appreciate and appraise the complexity of the human condition in its
conflicting values.

Unfortunately, Posner himself does not go quite this far. Indeed, after one has read Posner, one has to wonder if something
hasn't been valued. For instance, Posner has a series of comments
concerning family affairs which indicate that he has not fully
placed a value on some of the motivations inherent in this "institution":

> If love is (at its fullest) that state of feeling in which an increase in
> the loved one's utility or welfare increased the loving person's utility
> by the same amount, then in a marriage with full love the division
> of household income will be determined by the initial wealth en-
> dowments, rather than by the relative contributions of the partners.
> Love also reduces the costs of transactions within the family; it is a
> substitute for the hierarchical command relationships by which pro-
> duction is organized within the business firm as well as for the ex-
> plicit contractual relationship by which production is organized in
> the market.[32]

Or in speaking of children when Posner says

> Children may be produced (1) as an unintended by-product of sexual
> activity, (2) as an income-producing investment, (3) as a source of
> other services to the parents, and (4) (really a subset of [3]), out of
> an instinct or desire to preserve the species, or possibly to perpetuate
> the genetic characteristics, the name, or the memory of the
> parents.[33]

This is not the place to conduct an argument about whether
Posner's theses are moral any more than we wished to argue
whether or not the other scholars' theses were moral. When one
reads the above quotations, however, one has to wonder whether
economic analysis too blithely assumes or ignores the values of

emotion felt by humans. The point is that Posner is clearly incorrect in stating economic theory is the most promising theory of law, when the same theory cannot account for the depths of human behavior.

The arguments of Horwitz and Posner are powerful because they rely on a single analytical tool to explain law, and there is strength in simplicity. However, they are even more deficient than the argument of the economic historians, because they completely ignore anything that does not fit into a convenient economic pattern, or if they do attempt to fit it in, they badly distort the alien concept.

Stephen Presser and "Law and American History" (1980)

A major argument of this section has been that law cannot simply be forced into a single conceptual unit, unless that unit has the flexibility and sensitivity to account for the myriad complexity of the society that law mirrors. One scholar who has recognized this is Stephen Presser, who published the first contemporary American casebook on legal history. Presser's theory reaches beyond economic analysis to describe American legal history. His theory includes economics as well as religion, although he too occasionally limits religion to institutional affiliations. Nevertheless, his categorization of the themes of American law are quite harmonious with the themes of this section.

In the preface to *Law and American History*, Presser and his co-author, Jamil Zainaldin, describe their legal theory:

> We believe that American law . . . mirrors the social values of our culture, and that at any given time American law can also be seen to reflect the economic preferences or the political ideology of particular groups in the polity.[34]

The authors then state their four transcendent values of American legal history: 1) restraint of arbitrary power, 2) the ultimate political principle of popular sovereignty, 3) the primary purpose of the law being the furtherance of economic progress and social mobility, and 4) the support of private enterprise and individualism.[35]

These are broad values and are not dissimilar to the values advanced by the economic historians. What makes Presser's approach special is that his first step in understanding these values is in the context of religion. He begins the casebook by analyzing the competing religious values of King James I of England (1566–1625) and Sir Edward Coke (1552–1634) in their conception of the sources of the law. For James I the source of the law was the king because of the theological doctrine of the divine rights of kings that spoke of the idea of God speaking through his servant, the king. Coke believed that the source of the law was in the "artificial reason" of common law judges. These judges basically discovered the true law of nature and of God in the experience of the common law.

After this point, Presser often interjects questions of how the actors in the law actually view the sources of law and their authority within the law. Presser is sensitive to the religious orientation of the actors in the legal system as is reflected in some of his articles, one being his analysis of Judge John Thompson Nixon of New Jersey, whose Presbyterian faith influenced his jurisprudential substance and style.[36]

The insight of Presser is that questions of law carry with them questions of the values of society and those values are not determined solely upon economic grounds, although economic grounds will always be involved.

In classifying himself as a member of the "heroic school" of legal history, Presser says the members of this school recognize that man is after more than mere economic survival, but is also interested in spiritual and temporal salvation.[37] It is this sensitivity that gives Presser's analysis the depth and breadth that is vital for the accurate analysis of American legal history.

Conclusion

American legal history is not simply the story of economic development. Historians and philosophers who singularly dwell on the economic aspect of legal history normally have an accurate description of a part of American life, but inevitably fail to appreciate the complexity of the story. Perhaps the major reason for this failure is the insistence that religion is either an institutional creature or an ironclad set of rules. Both conceptions of religion fail to understand that religion in its fullest sense is an orientation, an understanding, and an experience of life with or without transcendental terminology. Religion, understood in this sense, has the focus to accurately analyze the story of American society, has the breadth to understand its vast complexity, and has the sensitivity to appreciate the deeper meanings of empirical data.

In the United States, the early settlers were interested in religious freedom, but part of their religion was economic gain. Until the Great Awakening of 1740, the dominant religion of America was Puritanism found primarily in Congregational and Presbyterian denominations. After the Great Awakening, America first experienced religious diversity within Calvinist denominations. The Calvinist theology continued to dominate American society even after Catholics and Jews broadened the membership of the country beyond Calvinist boundaries. During this period, the industrial revolution did deeply change American society and law. But the change toward the pursuit of economic growth and gain was anchored by a Calvinist notion of serving God in one's vocation and in reaping success as a sign of God's favor. Calvinism also did not remain stagnant, but expanded with the economic and philosophical developments of the times. It increased its confidence in humanity and consequently encouraged the freedom for individuals to grow.

Often, religious values do not conflict with each other for a long period of time. Such was the case when the twin forces of the Enlightenment and the publication of law reports forced common law judges to deal with contradictory rules under the whip of economic development. Such is also the case in our present society as the traditional values which condemn killing, abortion, and attacks on prayer meet head-on with values which permit tolerance of diverse religious groups. The contemporary American struggle is a battle of religious values.

This section does not attempt to argue for either side of the current religious debate. It does wish to suggest that it is a religious debate. Moreover, it wishes to show that because historians have failed to understand the religious nature of American society and American law, contemporary Americans have also failed to understand the sources of the current debate.

American legal history is the story of moralities interacting to produce law. The production of secular ethics from sacred ethics has not always been smooth, but Americans have always been able to create law without abandoning their religious identity. Having provided the philosophical and historical basis, I would like to develop an empirical application of theological categories to jurisprudential experiences.

PART III
JURISPRUDENCE OF FAITH:
USING THEOLOGY TO
INTERPRET JURISPRUDENCE

6. Theology in Connecticut Law

Any philosophical discussion tends to be somewhat vague, and in defining religion and law as ethical systems and as a way of life, the vagueness is exacerbated. While this book attempts to stretch the traditional concepts of law and religion, it also stands for the proposition that a basic Christian, even Calvinist way of life has dominated American history. The contemporary debate of church-state relations pits conflicting values within the traditional American/Christian perspective. One hopes, therefore, it would be constructive to look at other historical instances where competing values have conflicted to see how law and religion interact as well to see the methods used to resolve the conflict.

This section looks into the way of life of two Connecticut judges. Because of the nature of Connecticut prior to 1860, this question resolves itself into a question of the content of the judges' Christianity, and how that Christianity influenced their jurisprudence. It is important to remember Ellul's typology, particularly stages two and three.

The reader will remember that in stage two, natural law exists where law spontaneously arises from the mutual consensus of the people. In stage three, jurists and theoreticians begin to objectify the law by making law into a systematic theory, thereby making it a product of rational thought, rather than a spontaneously expressed set of values.

Connecticut was poised between stages two and three. In pre-1790 Connecticut, law was simply the Puritan way of life. The law was established by custom and legislation as a result of the political, economic and moral factors of the time. The established state church did not dictate the law, but the Puritan faith was so engrained in each person, that it was impossible for one to place himself outside of the Puritan way of life. However, this way of life was stable because of the unity of the people in the Puritan faith, a unity that was shattered by the Great Awakening of 1740. Those revivals diversified group conscience, driving conservative Congregationalists to the Methodist and Baptist churches and moderate Congregationalists to the Episcopal Church. Without a unified conscience, Connecticut law was pushed toward stage three, the systematic elaboration of the law. Connecticut only moved toward stage three however, it did not fully enter it.

Connecticut judges such as Zephania Swift and Tapping Reeve strove to rationally articulate the law and later justices followed their systematizing approach. But despite its rational technique, jurisprudence remained within the bounds of Christian thought. Religious preoccupation remained a way of life, and Connecticut was still guided by natural law as it was interpreted in a systematically Calvinist manner. Thus another theme of the section is that Connecticut moved from a natural law society toward a scientific law society because of the religious diversity spawned by the Great Awakening.

The primary way to understand the religious nature is to study two chief justices of the Connecticut Supreme Court of Errors. Zephania Swift and Tapping Reeve were the giants in transforming Connecticut jurisprudence and not so coincidentally, they served as chief justices during Connecticut's crucial decade of 1810 to 1820. Neither was hesitant to express his theology. Before turning to each one, however, a short sketch of Connecticut is needed to frame the context in which these judges worked.

Connecticut's first settlers were Puritans who emigrated from Massachusetts in 1636. Within a short time, Connecticut adopted the first modern constitution in the United States, the Connecticut Fundamental Orders. The Rev. Thomas Hooker, the most prominent personality in Connecticut, provided the substantive theory for the 1639 Constitution in a sermon given at the General Court on May 31, 1638.[1]

Hooker's sermon contained three main doctrines. First, that it was God's decision to allow people to choose their ruling magistrates. Second, that the enfranchised voters were to elect the magistrates according to what the people believed to be the will of God. Voting was not based on what the candidate could do for the individual voter, but on what the candidate could do for God. Third, that the people were to restrain the power of the incumbent magistrates. Election was not authority for monarchy or episcopacy. Underlying Hooker's doctrines was his explicit belief that people would be more inclined to love officers and give to them their obedience if the people freely elected them.[2]

Hooker's sermon illuminates the theological character of Connecticut civilization. Hooker, like John Calvin, stressed that God was not an aloof, disinterested being, but was an active participant in government. The entire political process was focused upon maximizing God's glory. This governmental focus on God accentuated the need for all of the society to have a consistent understanding of God's nature. As long as Connecticut enjoyed theological homogeneity, their theocentric government functioned effectively. However, this orientation also left Connecticut vulnerable to religious diversity, since diverse notions of God would directly attack the entire governmental structure.

The Fundamental Orders created a simple, but effective government which remained intact until the Connecticut Constitution of 1818. Written by a close friend of Hooker, Roger Ludlow, the Fundamental Orders provided for the election of six magistrates, who with a governor were to rule according to the will of God. Towns elected individual representatives who assisted these seven men and together they were known as the General Court, which possessed all judicial, legislative, and executive authority. In 1662, England recognized the provisions of the Fundamental Orders when it used them as the basis for granting Connecticut a charter which would remain Connecticut's official government document until the 1818 Constitution.

The Connecticut magistrates quickly recognized the necessity of delegating powers to inferior courts. By 1638, the General Court was appointing "assistants" to the judicially oriented inferior courts and made the local county courts extensions of its authority.[3] The lower courts mediated between persons, hearing civil cases that mainly dealt with property and probate issues. Debt actions were popular because they were inexpensive and because the lower court was often the only available forum in which the parties could bind their agreements. The lower courts also attracted a great number of personal morality cases which came in two groups. The first group consisted of prosecutions of offenses such as drunkenness, vulgarity, and sexual crimes. The second group concerned allegations against personal character such as slander and defamation.[4]

There are several good reasons for the numerous cases. First, the court was believed to be a God-given method of dispute resolution. The Puritans would not have hesitated to turn to the court to settle societal problems. Second, personal morality cases were not simply a secular affront, but a crucial religious issue. A person's piety was a sign of predestined salvific election. A slanderous remark directed against a person's reputation could call one's piety into doubt if the charge was left unmet. Thus, a slanderous statement could actually challenge the reality of one's eternal destiny. This is not a question of a personal affront, but of one's eternal self-understanding. Thus, legal courts were from the beginning based upon and concerned with issues that knew no dichotomy between concepts of secularity and sacredness.

In the one hundred years following the adoption of the Fundamental Orders, Puritan piety diminished. When this less intense piety was confronted with the increasing political, economic, and social complexity of the mid-1700s, the Great Awakening resulted. The Awakening, which exploded in 1740, was a religious revivalist movement that spread through most of the thirteen colonies and was particularly intense in New England. It shattered the religious unity of Connecticut. In its wake, the Great Awakening left a religiously diverse population that would not tolerate the presence of an established church and challenged the religious basis for the governance and jurisprudence of Connecticut. Before the Awakening, Connecticut was almost entirely Congregational; by 1776, one-third of the population had left the Congregational Church.[5]

The revivals were a Calvinist reassertion of the sovereignty of God and the depravity of man. The revivals fiercely objected to any diminution of the responsibilities of man to conduct a pious life and to any attempt to conceptualize man as enlightened. They emphasized the emotional conversion experience instead of professions of faith.[6] They were thought to be caused solely by an outpouring of God's spirit, so that it was thought that the more emotional one became at a revival, the more deeply one had been touched by the Holy Spirit.[7] They emphasized the participation of laity and the voluntary performance of moral acts. Attempts to enforce morality were disparaged.[8] Those who separated from the Congregational Church distrusted the Puritans because the Puritans were trying to enforce a lukewarm piety.

Because of the Great Awakening, there was no longer a religious homogeneity that had been the backbone of Connecticut government since the founding. Many moderate Congregationalists, fearing that their church might become ultraconservative, became Anglican and thus shaped the Anglican church into a Calvinist mold, while Baptist and Methodist congregations swelled, particularly in the rural areas.[9] Thus, it became much harder to view the members of the Assembly and the judges as expositors of God's will, since the methods of discovering God's will had changed. Diversity forced political and judicial institutions to find new methods of gaining and maintaining consensus and legitimacy. Connecticut moved toward a new stage, a stage where jurists rationally attempted to synthesize and systematize the old natural law. That new approach was the rational, scientific approach of Tapping Reeve and Zephania Swift.

The years 1790–1820 were years of political revolution and religious turbulence. Significant political forces triggered the adoption of a new constitution in 1818 that replaced the Charter of 1662 as the governing document of the state. There were two basic reasons for the desire for a new constitution, and both were based on religious motives.

First, there was the desire for religious liberty among the Episcopalians, the Methodists, and the Baptists, all of whom hated the certificate. The certificate allowed one to worship in his own church without having to pay taxes that supported the established Congregational Church. To receive a certificate, one had to apply directly to the legislature. The certificate allowed the Federalists/

Congregationalists to claim that Connecticut enjoyed religious freedom, but the dissenters found the tedious requirement of applying to the legislature an obnoxious limitation of religious liberty.[10] The politically astute state Republicans made the disestablishment of the Congregational Church and religious liberty primary party platforms and thereby snared the political allegiances of most of these religious dissenters.[11]

The second cause for the drive for the new constitution was the influence of the French Revolution. The Revolution stimulated the existing roots of religious discontent and also encouraged deism. The Great Awakening had already caused a deep religious split in Connecticut, and in the French-Indian War and the American Revolution, theologically vulnerable American soldiers were exposed to European deism and rationalism. Rationalism spurred a desire for Connecticut to erect a government with a new constitution. The deistic movement in the United States was spearheaded by Joseph Priestly, Ethan Allen, Thomas Paine, and Thomas Jefferson.

When the Connecticut Republicans criticized the Connecticut clergy, the Federalists quickly branded them as Jeffersonian, amoral deists. To the Federalist mind, any attack on the Congregational clergy was an attack on God. The Connecticut Federalists did not understand that the religious dissenters were Republican because that was the only way they could achieve religious freedom. The degree to which the political struggle was religiously based is revealed by Timothy Dwight's characterization of the Republicans as sabbath-breakers, profane swearers, attenders of amusements and balls, drunkards and gamblers.[12]

While several issues dominated the political scene from 1810–1820, the final issue which led to the Constitution was the problem of the distribution of war funds. Fourteen thousand dollars were due to Connecticut for its share of expenses of the War of 1812. In 1816, Connecticut received and distributed the money to the religious societies: one-third went to the Congregational Church, one-seventh went to the Bishop's Fund (Episcopal Church), one-twelfth went to the Methodist Church, one-eighth went to the Baptist Church, one-seventh went to Yale, and the remainder went into the state treasury.[13] The allocation angered everybody. The Congregationalists felt that they deserved more, and the others felt that the Congregationalists had unfairly benefited. It inflamed the religious pluralism problem even more.

The 1817 election focused on church-state separation, religious tests for office, secret handling of state finances, taxation, and the Hartford Convention. (The Hartford Convention was held in 1814. It almost led to the secession of Connecticut and Massachusetts from the Union and was quickly branded a traitorous gathering.) None of these issues were particularly favorable to the Federalists. The result was that the Republicans, who were also (significantly) known as the Tolerationists, won the 1817 gubernatorial election by six hundred votes, and won control of the General Assembly.[14]

The 1818 Convention was generally composed of religiously tolerant delegates. It was a nonpartisan meeting since the Federalists went along with the Republican reforms. The three major innovations in the new constitution were that religious toleration was granted to all Christians, the government was divided into three branches, and the Congregational Church was disestablished.[15] While the political resolution of religious pluralism was the Constitution, Connecticut turned to a familiar movement, the revival, for the religious solution.

From 1800 to 1830, Connecticut experienced an almost continuous state of revivalism which emphasized humanitarian activity. While Calvinism had always encouraged ethical responsibility, these revivals differed in that the activity was geared toward the development of the social good. The revivals cut across denominational lines and sparked formation of missionary societies; bible, tract, and educational societies; Sunday schools; and other societies for moral reform.[16] The Connecticut Bible Society was founded in 1811 to send Bibles to the Western frontier. The Connecticut Society for the Promotion of Good Morals was founded to further "moral" sermons and inveighed against intemperateness. The Domestic Mission Society for Connecticut and Vicinity was founded to build up "waste places" and the New England Tract Society established a school for the deaf and dumb.[17]

The theological focus of the revivals, as in Calvinism and the Great Awakening, was the grace and power of God, and the need for human submission to the will of God. These revivals, however, added two significant innovative thoughts to Calvinism: the value of the individual and the social responsibility of the church. The church was no longer to serve merely as a place for the gathering of the elect, but it was to be concerned about the common good. The individual was no longer depraved but had some intrinsic worth. This new shift deemphasized the doctrines of election and predestination; man had responsibilities and control over his ultimate destiny.[18] He was no longer simply a pawn in supernatural hands.

The humanitarian emphasis was able to cut through denominational divisions. It was easier to build consensus about the rightness of sending Bibles to the West than it was to determine the nature of original sin. The emphasis on humanitarianism entailed a higher understanding of the nature of man. But this "improved" man was still sinful and in need of God's grace, so that while the revivalist theology viewed man more sympathetically, he was not considered to be a perfectable being.

Rationalism also broadened consensus. Instead of following Puritan law, all law was subject to examination, explanation, and systemization. By 1789, Connecticut was using written reports of judicial opinions, the first American state to do so.[19] The written reports required the judge to base his opinions on logical argument instead of notions of custom and experience. The natural law was no longer sufficient to hold consensus, and rational law took its place. This new emphasis on logical systemization and argument was pioneered by Tapping Reeve and Zephania Swift.

7. Tapping Reeve

Tapping Reeve's contribution to Connecticut jurisprudence cannot be overstated. He established America's first formal law school in Litchfield, Connecticut. He published some of the earliest legal treatises on American law, and was chief justice of the Connecticut Supreme Court. He consistently attempted to rationally and systematically articulate the law. His articulation was a direct outgrowth of his theology, for he felt that the law was systematized religious truth.

Reeve's jurisprudence can best be grasped by understanding as much of the man as is possible. First, his way of life will be examined. This means looking at Reeve's lifestyle, his activities, his politics, and his theological orientation. Then his legal theory will be presented while simultaneously noting how that theory was theological.

Quite simply, Tapping Reeve's entire existence revolved around his religion.

> Reeve's public and private life was under the domination of religion, a religion which was strengthened by the most sublime and comprehensive view of God, His character, law, gospel, and government in all its unerring rectitude and great results . . . Reeve chose to live a religion which was ardent, but not given to open enthusiasm. The characteristic traits of his piety were ardour, constancy, humility, and gratitude.[1]

Reeve's social humanitarianism was extensive. He was the president of the Connecticut Bible Society, whose purpose it was to send Bibles to the western frontier. He was vice-president of the

Connecticut Society for the Promotion of Good Morals, which was founded to further "moral" sermons and which inveighed against intemperateness. He was a close friend of the most prominent revivalist of the early nineteenth century, Lyman Beecher, and enthusiastically embraced Beecher's calls for greater humanitarian activities. In his personal life he was self-effacing, humble, and loyal. His personality was such that one of his law students wrote that "no instructor was ever more generally loved by his pupils."[2] Yet Reeve's humility did not entail any wavering about the rightness of his faith or the wrongness of other faiths, as shown by his willingness to stand against members of his own family. His lifestyle was rather antipodal to that of his cosmopolitan brother-in-law, Aaron Burr, and Reeve spurned all of the former vice-president's attempts to contact him.[3] It has also been suggested that Reeve's fierce piety was a reaction to the debacle of his father, a Presbyterian minister, who was dismissed by his congregation for perpetual drunkenness.[4]

Whatever the family reasons, there is no doubt that Reeve clearly saw a difference between the righteousness of his faith and the darkness of the faith of others. Reeve said that those who were not members of his faith were "fellow sinners [who were] groping in the more than midnight gloom of heathen darkness."[5] Reeve, an ardent Federalist, denigrated the integrity of the Republicans by saying that they were not serious about their ideological beliefs (meaning the desire for religious liberty), but were merely politically ambitious.[6] To Reeve, the Republican movement was an effort to prepare Connecticut for a revolution that would knife the heart of religious, governmental, and social being.[7]

How could Reeve humbly live a life as the exemplary do-gooder and at the same time stubbornly reject the ways of life variant to his own, even to the point of completely misunderstanding Methodist, Episcopal, and Baptist desires for religious liberty? Politics and ethics, like laws, are important indicia of orientation, but politics and ethics understood as acts often do not illuminate the deeper, underlying forces which orient life. Thus, just as to understand the law we must delve into the way of life of the justice instead of confining ourselves to laws and traditional institutions of religion, so for the justice we must dig beneath politics and ethics to understand his way of life, or more correctly, we must understand that ethics are a broader way of life.

Tapping Reeve was not an innovative theologian, nor is there any hint that he ever desired or claimed to be. Yet his theological statements, activities, and relationships tie him to three of the greatest theologians in New England history. He lived in the same town and was a friend of Lyman Beecher, he was allied with Yale President Timothy Dwight, and he was married to the granddaughter of Jonathan Edwards. These three men had enormous influence in Connecticut life from 1740 to 1830 by articulating and shaping the predominant intellectual theology to which Tapping Reeve so faithfully adhered.

The fundamental notions of this Connecticut orthodoxy was that man was totally depraved and that God was totally powerful and good. The statements of these themes would vary. Edwards would insist that man was sinful because Adam's original sin was imputed to all men, an Augustinian notion, while Beecher accepted a Taylorist notion that man was sinful simply because each man sinned. There was a rejection of any Arminian tendency to argue that man somehow had a role in his own salvation. Man was depraved; whatever was good came from God, an idea that Reeve articulated in a letter in 1812 when he spoke of Connecticut education:

> Our hands ought to rise in gratitude (to God) in an especial manner for the distinguishing pleasure of having our education under the sunshine of the gospel.[8]

Reeve simply restated the Puritan thought that if all good, including the government, came from God, then any attack on those "good" things was an attack on Reeve's God and had to be fought. Reeve believed in a somber, serious appropriation of God, an appropriation that the more charismatic Baptists and Methodists did not share. The Baptists and Methodists were passionate worshippers similar to the emotional worshippers during the Great Awakening. Reeve believed that

> Passion, so far as it prevails, destroys reason, and when it gains entire ascendency over men, it renders them bedlamites.[9]

Thus Reeve's conception of God and his understanding of how man communicated with God drove him away from the religious dissenters who were a part of the Republican Party. Since the primary political question of the time was religious liberty and disestablishment, Reeve and the religious dissenters were squarely at odds. The political questions directly undermined Connecticut's (and Reeve's) God, government, religion, and society and it did so precisely because it was not simply a political challenge, but a theological one.

Reeve thus found himself straddling two understandings of religion in which there was a tension. Anthropologically, liturgically, and politically there was a wide chasm between Reeve and the religious dissenters, a chasm that led him to oppose the idea of accepting religious pluralism. He could therefore be exclusive; he could shun Aaron Burr and his father, and label the Republicans as selfish bedlamites. But the forces which attacked his religion were also forcing the religion to redefine itself in populist tendencies. Had there not been a pluralist society challenging the Congregational Church it is doubtful that a Lyman Beecher could spark a humanitarian movement. Thus Reeve was also a part of a religion that unconsciously, but implicitly, was accepting religious diversity. Reeve exemplified that by his humanitarian activities, and through the method that he brought to jurisprudence. The varying moralities of diverse Connecticut forced law to change by becoming more rational and more humanitarian. These secular ethical changes, accepted by Reeve, in turn impacted upon his religion, making it more humanitarian and rational. Of course each factor in turn reimpacted upon other factors. Reeve preserved his theology, but altered it enough to be in alignment with a diverse society.

The single most important aspect of Tapping Reeve's theory of law was that it was religious. Justice Samuel Church, who would follow Reeve as Connecticut's Chief Justice in 1847, said that Reeve

> loved the law as a science, and studied it philosophically. He considered it as the practical application of religious principles. He wished to reduce it to a certain symmetrical system of moral truth.[10]

What Reeve did was to take his and Connecticut's religious experience, which encompassed the totality of life, and give it a structured, systematic, rational expression. Essentially Reeve was creating a "scientific jurisprudence" in that he made the law rationally structured and in a sense objective. The law was not objective because it was politically or cosmologically neutral, an impossible status, but because it reached a centrality of consensus among Connecticut's new diversity. It is important to remember that while the Connecticut religious landscape was no longer simply Congregational, and while the Enlightenment had stimulated Arminianism, all of the denominations were still Calvinist. Reeve basically introduced a Calvinist, systematic jurisprudence, a stage that conformed to Ellul's stage three where the law is rationally articulated and systematically synthesized as part of an intellectual, political, and jurisprudential theory, whereas in Puritan Connecticut, the judge was trusted because he was the interpreter of the will of God. Now the judge would be trusted because he could articulate the reasons for a decision in a logic independent of Congregational orthodox faith.

Reeve introduced "scientific jurisprudence" in three ways. The most dramatic was his opening of the Litchfield Law School, the first of its kind in the nation. There, students underwent a systematic, formal training in the law. Second, Reeve wrote several of the earliest American legal treatises in which he surveyed the entire field of law, enunciated the governing principles of the area, and derived the applications from the principles. Finally, he wrote his judicial opinions, a relatively new exercise in American courts. In his opinions, Reeve insisted upon a strict adherence to the use of proper forms and suits.

Much of Reeve's jurisprudence seems absolutely dull, as there is nothing that strikes the modern eye as either innovative or excessively arcane. For instance, in *Sacket v. Mead*,[11] the defendant was the administrator of an insolvent estate. The creditors had been paid off to the extent possible and the statute of limitations for their further payment had elapsed. The defendant then showed some other estate property to the plaintiff, who was also a creditor of the estate. Under the applicable statute, once the statute of limitations had elapsed, the creditors could not receive further payments unless the creditors could show further estate property. The plaintiff claimed that the defendant had done so, but also claimed that he was entitled to have his claim fully satisfied to the exclusion of the other creditors.

Reeve, who did not write the majority opinion, refused to allow the creditor to recover his full payment because such payment defeated the principle of average. Reeve found the principle in the applicable statute and insisted that if any distribution was made, it had to be made in shares to all the creditors. Further, Reeve would not allow a suit until the commissioners who would have been appointed to oversee the administration of an insolvent estate had met to strike this particular estate average. Reeve said that the plaintiff could maintain a suit on the defendant's probate bond, and then the proceeds of the bond would be distributed fairly to the creditors.

In his adjudication of *Sacket*, Reeve relied on the principle of average, on the necessity to bring a suit on the defendant's probate bond instead of a suit against the estate for prompt distribution, and on the tradition of deferring to the legislature. None of this was scriptural, nothing was innovative, but all was a continuation of the Puritan past. But because it was an open, logical presentation of the past, it was socially acceptable. Reeve was far too committed to his Puritan past, liturgically and legally, to alter it. But the method he chose to articulate the past, through humanitarian activity and scientific jurisprudence, was a method that was broader than the past. A hint to the humanitarian aspect of Reeve comes through in *Grumon v. Raymond and Betts.*[12]

In *Grumon* the justice of the peace of Fairfield County issued a search warrant for stolen goods. The warrant authorized the sheriff to "search . . . suspected places, houses, stores, or barns in said (town of) Wilton. . . ." Sheriff Betts falsely arrested Grumon and four others. Grumon sued for trespass *vi et armis*. The defendant justice of the peace argued that he was immune from suit since he was acting in his judicial capacity. He also argued that while he might have erred in his issuance of the warrant, it was not an irregular process. He also argued that the only person actually liable was the person who made the arrest — the sheriff.

The court held that the justice of the peace was liable for the issuance of a general warrant. Reeve said that there were several requisites for a proper search warrant, among them being that the stolen articles were in a specific place. Reeve said that a justice was not liable if he issued a warrant which was recognized, but was invalid because of some mistake, but when a judge issued a warrant that the law did not recognize, as was the case here, then the justice was potentially liable.

Besides imposing a burden of care on justices of the peace, thereby making them subservient to the processes of the law, the *Grumon* opinion respects the individual. An individual could not be subjected to harassment from governmental officials because the individual himself was worthy of protection. The restraint of governmental power was not dependent upon revivalist humanitarianism for its existence. Puritan Connecticut would probably have nodded with approval Reeve's reasoning and result. But the fact that the reasoning was now publicly articulated in written form broadened its acceptance beyond Puritan boundaries. Reeve consistently followed his *Grumon* and *Sacket* approach of presenting Puritan law through broader methodology. In content, the value of the individual was fully in line with the theological concepts of revivalist Connecticut.

In Reeve's *The Law of Baron and Femme*, he again revealed the importance of his Puritan past. In stating that "few maxims of our law are more important than that of stare decisis,"[13] Reeve showed his veneration of the past. His treatise shows the intertwining of law and religion more explicitly than his opinions. For instance, Reeve said that parents had the duty to provide "instruction of them [children] in reading their own language, so as to be able to search the scripture and learn the revealed will of God."[14] This was necessary in order that the children learn the capital offenses of the state. Reeve discerned that it was part of the law to teach children to learn scripture, and scripture was necessary to understand the law. To understand Connecticut marriage law, one had to understand the Bible since "all marriages forbidden by God's law or within the Levitical degrees of kindred are invalid."[15]

Reeve did not view theology and law as distinct principles. He was primarily interested in articulating them consonant with his religious/legal moorings. However, his way of life had already begun to move away from the Puritan orthodoxy because of the new religious pluralism. Thus the method Reeve used to live out his theology was a method which had interdenominational appeal both in religious humanitarian endeavors and in legal scientific jurisprudence. Tapping Reeve had simply grown with his religious environment. The old Puritan morality, expressed secularly in a magesterial system of government under terms of depraved humanity gave way to an ethic which found humanitarianism and logic to be an effective way of life in pluralistic Connecticut. Reeve was not forced to accept the morality of the religious dissenters; they formed law which was humanitarian, logical, and which generally perpetuated the Puritan past. In circular fashion, this secular ethic changed Reeve's morality so his individual faith also incorporated into itself humanitarianism and logic. For Reeve, law was much more than a tool responsive to economic changes; rather, economic, along with political, religious, and other social changes challenged Connecticut's way of life. Reeve's life, from family relations to politics and to jurisprudence was a response to justify history and simultaneously adapt to a new secular and sacred ethic.

8. Zephania Swift

Zephania Swift was probably the most influential person in Connecticut law. He wrote the first legal treatises in the United States, which were enormously influential in Connecticut and elsewhere. While in the United States House of Representatives, he wrote his first treatise — *A System of Laws of the State of Connecticut*. In 1810, he wrote his *Digest of the Laws of Evidence*. He was appointed to the state Supreme Court and was thereafter elected to chief justice replacing Tapping Reeve. After retiring from the Supreme Court, Swift wrote his *Digest of the Laws of Connecticut*. He died in 1823.[1]

Swift rationally systematized everything. Theologically he insisted upon a rational deism free from ecclesiastical rigidity, open to religious pluralism, and based upon a very structured, ordered universe. Jurisprudentially, he also stressed finding central principles and systematic application of those principles.

In sketching Tapping Reeve's life, it was most convenient to first appreciate Reeve's deeds and then proceed to his stated thoughts concerning religion. The crux of Reeve's theology was in his actions; with Swift, it was in his words, a statement which in no way is designed to disparage his religion. Swift simply took the time to publicly detail his theology. Thus the logical starting point for Swift is his expressed theology.

Swift's theology was less rigid than Reeve's. Reeve basically embraced Puritan theology as modified by the revivals. Swift's theology was also shaped by the revivals' humanitarian spirit, but was also strongly shaped by the rationalism of the Enlightenment. These twin influences shaped Swift into a deist, but a deist who refuted the ideas of many contemporary deists such as Thomas Paine. Interestingly, Swift's theology bore a character remarkably similar to the theology of John Calvin. Swift said that he was a follower of Christ and was "desirous only to strip his gospel of the conventional additions of ecclesiasticism, and show it divine in form as it originally stood."[2]

Opposing some contemporary rationalists, Swift first established that there indeed was a God. Swift felt that any rational person had to believe in God:

> The being of God is so universally impressed on the human mind, that it seems unnecessary to guard against a denial of it by human laws. Atheism is too cold and comfortless to be a subject of popular belief.[3]

Swift's language is similar to Calvin's reasoning for the knowledge of God. Calvin stated that

> There exists in the human mind, and indeed by natural instinct, some sense of Deity, we hold to be beyond dispute, since God himself, to prevent any man from pretending ignorance has endued all men with some idea of his Godhead . . . There is no notion so barbarous, no race so brutish, as not to be imbued with the conviction that there is a God.[4]

In both statements, there was a strong belief that one believes in God simply because it was a natural, rational thing for humans to do. The utility of this basic method of proof of God was that it allowed constant appeal to reason for ethical and ecclesiastical theory because it was through reason that humans became aware of God.

Swift rejected the idea of a vindictive God who was often presented in sermons of "fire and brimstone," but thought of God as "a kind parent."[5] This description of God rings of Calvin, who said that by accepting Christ, one of the resulting benefits for Christians was that God was transformed from a judge into an indulgent father.[6]

Not only did Swift displace the idea of a vindictive God, he also distanced God from everyday life. The most revealing way he

did this was through the names he gave to God. Swift used amorphous terms such as Supreme Deity and Supreme Character to
name God. His names were indicative of a deism which recognized
God as a creator, but not as a closely personal God. Swift needed
some way to describe the connection between God and humanity,
for if he left his theology as it had been described so far, humans
would have little need to consider an aloof, amorphous God.
Swift's link was logical reason.

Logical reason structured Swift's cosmology, his scriptural interpretation, his philosophy of Christianity, and his ethics.
Cosmologically, the world was a rationally structured system. He
said that the Supreme Deity

> . . . has created innumerable systems of worlds—peopled them with
> an infinite variety of inhabitants, and governs by general and im-
> mutable laws—that in universal nature, he has established the best
> possible system for the general good . . . this world is but a small part
> of the great plan . . . [and] this life is but a commencement of an ex-
> istence which shall never end.[7]

Scripturally, he interpreted the Bible so it was consistent with
reason. Swift said that

> certainly no construction should be put on the language of our
> Savior, that would make him promulgate a doctrine wholly inconsis-
> tent with reason and justice.[8]

Swift also said that Christianity was nothing more than reason and
common sense.

> In its uncorrupted state, Christianity is unquestionably, not only
> consistent with, but founded on the dictates of reason and common
> sense.[9]

He objected to a church-centered religion and a church-centered
state. He felt that the clergy had overstepped its proper role, even
beyond the excesses of the Roman church.[10] He felt that the Congregational Church had assumed too much power, power that had
corrupted Christianity. Thus, Swift was not a supporter of the

religious predominance of the Puritans and fully accepted Connecticut's religious diversity. He felt that the practical application of religion was much more important than proofs of the absolute rightness of any one denomination. Swift's desire for practical application of religion placed him in step with the humanitarian revivals. For Swift, Christian ethics were based on the example of the Good Samaritan:

> What doctrine can be more sublime and worthy the divine character of our Savior, than to teach us the duty to exercise humanity and compassion to all that are in distress, without regard to sect, religion, or nation. Yet, how many people may be found among them who call themselves Christians, who think there is more merit in making one long prayer, than in the noble exercise of humanity as in the case of the Samaritan.[11]

Thus Swift wanted an ethical way which was true to Christianity but which transcended denominationalism. He wanted a church which was true to Christianity and not obsessed with power, prestige, or ultimate predominance. The way to do this was to use reason, to describe, to interpret scripture, and to understand Christianity itself. His method was that of a rationalist who accepted religious pluralism and who rejected Puritan hegemony. It was a method which transcended denominationalism. Most of all, it was a method based on the same structured rationality that Swift would implement in his jurisprudence.

Given Swift's perspective of rational structure, it is not surprising that he was insistent upon the proper understanding of the role of Connecticut's Supreme Court. In fact Swift said that the most painful occurrence of his life involved a dispute over the definition of the role of the Supreme Court.[12] Because it was such an important event, and since it reveals some of Swift's governmental presuppositions, the story of the Peter Lung trial is worth retelling.

Lung was accused of murdering his wife. At the time, the Superior Court was not in session, so Swift ordered a special court although he had no explicit statutory authority. Swift felt that he needed to convene the court immediately because of the threat of witness tampering, because one of the witnesses was near death, and because he simply desired to conduct a speedy trial. Lung's counsel did not object to the special court and Lung was convicted of murder. The community then felt compassion for Lung, and his case was appealed to the legislature. The legislature annulled the action of Swift's court, viewing the proceeding as extrajudicial and void.[13] Swift said that if he had improperly convened the court, with a resulting death sentence, then he had committed a criminal act.[14]

Swift had four arguments against the Assembly's action. He cited a statute which allowed the chief justice to call a special court on "extraordinary circumstances." He appealed to common sense. He claimed that previous chief justices had also convened a special court. Finally, he said that Lung did not ask for a new trial, which the legislature gave to him, but for a pardon.[15]

Swift gave several reasons why it was a mistake to allow the legislature to interfere with the judiciary. He first cited the experience of judges.

> [J]udges have formed opinions on the whole science of jurisprudence, and heretofore it has been understood that the more law learning a man had, the better qualified he was to be a judge.[16]

He also said that the power assumed by the legislature gave it the discretion to overturn any court, a power which could be used for evil by corrupt men. The only restraint on the legislature, moral sentiment, was not enough. Allowing the legislature to interfere with the judiciary would lead to uncertainty, endless appeal, and was an invitation to despotism because the legislature was unrestrained by legal principles and vulnerable to being duped.[17]

Instead of allowing ultimate appeal to the legislature, Swift said that

> The tribunal of dernier resort should be composed of men qualified by their integrity, talents, science, and experience ... and should be rendered independent of popular whim and clamour.[18]

Swift said that judicial independence was "essential to the due and impartial administration of justice."[19]

The Peter Lung controversy revealed Swift's concern for

having carefully defined governmental function, but it more deeply revealed some preconceptions that were not historically valid. Swift's complaint of legislative interference in judicial functioning assumed that the legislative and judicial branches were separate and ignored the fact that the Fundamental Orders made them indivisible. Because the legislature had delegated judicial authority to the court, the Supreme Court had developed an image of itself as the court of last appeal, an image which correlated with the American federal system. Swift was not able to efficaciously implement his theological and jurisprudential rationalism if the court was not properly structured as independent; that independence, however, was not envisioned by the Fundamental Orders.

The nature of law was spelled out in Swift's *Digest of the Laws of the State of Connecticut*:

> The science of the law is grounded on certain first principles existing in the nature and fitness of things. These have been introduced by the statutes of the legislature, or have been derived from the dictates of reason—from considerations of policy—from the excellent maxim of civil law, to live virtuously, injure nobody and to render to every man his due—and from the sublime precept of Christian morality, to do to others as we would they should do to us.[20]

In Swift's system, the world was part of a greater divine, universal system. Within this world, law was founded on the nature of things and expressed in several sources. Swift attempted to discover these universal principles, principles that were religious because of their place in Swift's cosmology. He then attempted to apply those principles to the particular circumstances of the case.

Chapman v. Gillett[21] and *Fox v. Abel*[22] showed the explicit interrelationship between institutional religion and law in Swift's Connecticut. In *Chapman*, Chapman had given testimony before a meeting of a Presbyterian church. Gillett charged that Chapman had committed perjury. Chapman sued Gillett for defamation of character and claimed that the words "charging perjury" were themselves actionable. Chapman's oath had been administered by a justice of the peace.

Swift held that the words were actionable because alleging a perjury at a church meeting was the same as alleging a perjury at any other judicial forum. Swift stated that ecclesiastical tribunals were "necessary, not only for the promotion of religion, but for the peace and well-being of society"[23] Ecclesiastical tribunals "may be said to be courts where justice is judicially administered."[24] Swift said that to find justice, a tribunal must be empowered to administer an oath, and than he extended the rules of actionable slander to include ecclesiastical tribunals:

> It has been decided in the Court, that to charge a man with perjury before arbitrators, is actionable slander; and now, by analogy, we extend the same principle to ecclesiastical tribunals.[25]

For a man who excoriated the influence of the church in government, such a broad extension of authority to an ecclesiastical body is curious. While Swift did not want a clergy-dominated state, he was apparently willing and anxious to have the churches share in the administration of government. If he had wanted religion completely out of government, it would have been quite easy for him to refuse to extend the rule of actionable slander, but his opinions reveal unwillingness to separate Christianity from government. In the first sentence of the opinion, he declared that "Christianity is the law of the land."

Swift wanted a continuation of the past, and thus sanctioned religious tribunals. But the approach he used was systematic law. He kept law in its Christian context, but pushed the methodology toward Ellul's stage three where jurists attempt to systematize the law.

In *Fox*, the court was called upon to determine the length of the Sabbath. The Constable (Abel) arrested Fox on the morning of a Sunday, but before dawn. A statute prohibited arrests on Sunday. Fox sued Abel for trespass *vi et armis*. The court had to decide what time period was meant by "Sabbath."

All of the judges wrote opinions on the issue. Swift felt that the Sabbath included more than the solar day, which would enable Fox to enforce the statute and sue Abel. Swift based his opinion on Blackstone's Commentaries and English law which generally described the contours of a day. The other justices took a variety of approaches. Trumbull immediately cited Leviticus, Matthew, and Mark. Smith felt that only the statute should be examined, not scripture, England, or the common law. Brainard based his decision on the Decalogue and Christianity's interpretation of the statute. Hosmer relied on what he felt was normal Christian usage.

Just as Swift objected to theological hairsplitting among churches, so he avoided a religious debate in *Fox*. Instead of making a Puritan move to appeal to scripture, he appealed to secular treatises. *Fox* shows that the same judge who in *Chapman* incorporated Christianity into law and government insisted upon adjudicating a case on a systematic method. The methodology had become broader than scriptural interpretation, just as Connecticut religion had become broader than a single denomination.

The interface of religion and law can also be seen in Swift's treatment of crimes against religion. Swift felt that the Supreme Deity was perfectly capable of avenging his holy law without help from the judiciary. Crimes against religion could be punished only when they simultaneously offended religion and the "happiness of civil society."[26] There was a tension in this philosophy, however, because what offended the "happiness of civil society" was dependent upon the level of theological unanimity in the state. Thus blasphemy, atheism, polytheism, Unitarianism and profane swearing were punishable crimes only because Connecticut was still a religious state. Heresy and Judaism were not punishable in large measure because of the tolerance of religious diversity.

This tension is also seen in Swift's consideration of oaths. Swift said that the oath was "based on 1) moral obligation to speak truth and remorse of conscience for violation and 2) knowledge of God and future rewards and punishments."[27] Thus, as long as one recognized the obligation of an oath to tell the truth and understood the transcendental results of the failure to tell the truth, one could be a witness.

Swift also said that what a person believed and said about an oath and its underlying basis was not hearsay, but a simple fact. Thus if a person did not believe in the transcendental effects of lying, his statements could be used as facts to undermine his admissibility as a witness. But a man could not be forced to reveal his opinions about God in court.[28]

Swift thus left the oath question in a quandary. If a person kept his mouth shut about his beliefs, then his beliefs could not be questioned and he could be a witness. But, if the witness had made any statement which showed disbelief in either the obligation to tell the truth or of the transcendental effects of the failure to tell the truth, he could be dismissed. This was a very restrictive understanding of freedom of speech and religion. Swift effectively safeguarded religious expression as long as it agreed with his theology. Swift differed from the Puritans only in the degree to which he allowed religious freedom.

Swift's conception of all religious elements was that of an ordered reason and that reason was the tool Swift used to shape his life, particularly his jurisprudence. His acceptance of diversity and of the humanitarian spirit also led him to an insistence upon Christian ethics devoid of sectarian competition. His entire theology was one which transcended denominationalism, but which remained Christian. Like Reeve, he embraced a secular ethic based on logic and humanitarianism, but that embrace sometimes led to a strange combination of jurisprudential content.

In taking law toward scientific jurisprudence, Swift went a step beyond Reeve. Reeve trusted the religious monopoly of the Congregationalists and was more willing to turn to scripture to support his treatise law. He followed the forces of religious pluralism to emphasize scientific law and humanitarianism, but he did not fully support diversity. Swift's way of life fully supported diversity and rationalism and not coincidentally he more fully developed his scientific jurisprudence. There was a direct relationship between the acceptance of pluralism and the development of scientific law. Yet, even Swift was unable to completely break from the natural law of the past.

After Swift, the Connecticut jurisprudence was delicately poised between its inherited natural law and its scientific law. The overwhelming Christian/Calvinist nature of Connecticut prevented Reeve and Swift from dissociating religion from law. But the pluralism also drove the law to the unifying scientific jurisprudence. Connecticut law was scientific within a Calvinist context.

Two Supreme Court justices, Tapping Reeve and Zephania Swift, adjudicated in a climate of transition from monolithic

Puritanism to pluralistic Calvinism. Because of the religious tensions of the day, they sought to bring a legitimate method of dispute resolution to the court. For both men, that method was scientific jurisprudence, which itself was centered on man's ability to reason, which was a direct expression of their theologies. The transformation of Connecticut law was reflective of, and dependent upon, the religious developments of pluralism, rationalism, and humanitarianism in Connecticut society.

Both men inherited a Calvinist theology although each had slightly different perspectives of that Calvinism. Because of Connecticut's emerging pluralism, both men simultaneously followed and led the development of law based upon scientific jurisprudence, humanitarianism, and religious toleration. That secular ethic influenced change in the moral code adopted by each. For both, the change in law was not simply economic instrumentalism, but a change based on a change of an entire way of life.

PART IV
THE MODERN DEBATE

9. Jerry Falwell
and the Fundamentalists

This book has occasionally referred to a modern debate of the relationship of religion and law. This debate is being conducted in academic realms, in religious circles, and in the political arena. Not only is there a debate between atheists and theists concerning the role of religion in public life, but between theists themselves in defining the appropriate role for religion. For instance, Governor Mario Cuomo and Reverend Jerry Falwell have espoused very different conceptions of the role that religion should play in law and politics. These two individuals approach the issue from quite different perspectives. Falwell's argument is a continuation of the American revivalist spirit of the Great Awakening and the less emotional, but nonetheless effective, revivals of the early 1800s. The current revivalism directly pits sacred against secular ethics.

Jerry Falwell and his Moral Majority have had a significant impact upon American politics and upon law itself. Like Jacques Ellul, Falwell grounds his philosophy in a very specific, Calvinist understanding of the world. As with Ellul's approach, there is a tremendous strength in Falwell's perspective, but there are also weaknesses which undermine the applicability of his theology to the American situation. It is important to understand why Falwell thinks America has been great, what role he thinks the Bible should play in the creation of law, his understanding of how America has decayed, and his understanding of the relationship of church and state.

Falwell, Calvin, and Ellul agree that God is an all-powerful active being who ultimately controls government, not in the sense that good or evil governments do what God commands them, but by the fact that God ordains all governments, who then have the freedom and the responsibility to act for or against God.[1] In noting that "[O]ur Founding Fathers were not all Christians, but they were guided by biblical principles," Falwell argues that the underlying cornerstone of the United States was the wisdom distilled from God's word.[2] Thus, we have men like Tapping Reeve, who found great comfort and confidence in grounding law in religion; Zephania Swift, who deemphasized the explicit religious underpinning of law while enforcing and perpetuating the same principles in a broader manner; and Thomas Paine, who wanted nothing to do with religion but found that religious and patriotic principles amounted to many of the same things, were undergirded by divine wisdom.

While Falwell, like the economic historians, recognizes that many of the early laws regarding sexuality and Sabbath observance were religiously based, he also proclaims that much broader laws, or ways of life, were and are specifically mandated by the Bible:

> The free-enterprise system is clearly outlined in the Book of Proverbs in the Bible. Jesus Christ made it clear that the work ethic was a part of His plan for man. Ownership of property is biblical. Competition in business is biblical. Ambitious and successful business management is clearly outlined as a part of God's plan for His People.[3]

This far-reaching understanding of biblical guidance provides Falwell with a broad and powerful base to attack immoral statutes and national movements which conflict with early American life. If the founding fathers grounded America's law on infallible biblical principles, and if America is great because God blesses those who are faithful to the Bible, then it is logical that Falwell should warn America that it is jeopardizing its greatness with the risk of political, economic, and military instability.

To paraphrase Falwell, America has removed God from secular ethics and given its trust to government.[4] Expecting government to be the solution of human problems is the result of confidence in the ability of humans to create solutions independent of divine activity. This confidence, "humanism," defined as

> a doctrine, attitude, or way of life centered on human interests or values; a philosophy that asserts the dignity and worth of man and his capacity for self-realization through reason and that often rejects supernaturalism . . . [5]

is a major, if not the major force that is driving Americans away from God and the Bible. Existential humanism is itself objectionable, because it centers on human, not godly values, and since it assumes that humans can reach some sort of meaningful existence apart from God.

Falwell writes that this secular humanism has become a religion which has spawned and sustained its own value system. It has rejected the laws and the ethics of the Bible:

> Humanists believe that man is his own god and that moral values are relative, that ethics are situational. Humanists say that the Ten Commandments and other moral and ethical laws are outmoded and hindrances to human progress. [6]

Falwell argues that the public educational system instills these values in children. Instead of being taught the lessons and wisdom of the Bible, students are instructed to develop and learn human solutions to social and scientific problems of the world. Humanism thus attacks both the educational system and the traditional family so that the biblical wisdom which made the United States great is ignored. Falwell sums up the problems of the American educational system when he says that:

> The fear of the Lord is the beginning of knowledge (Proverbs 1:7). I believe that the decay in our public school system suffered an enormous acceleration when prayer and Bible reading were taken out of the classroom by the U.S. Supreme Court. Our public school system is now permeated with humanism. The human mind has now been deceived, and the end result is that our schools are in serious trouble. [7]

It is clear that Falwell believes that the rise of humanism has led to the decline of America. His analysis is directly related to his understanding of the relationship of church and state, religion and law, Christianity and politics. Falwell rejects the notion that religion and law are separated because humanism is the current state religion. Thus, the question for Falwell is not whether or not the state is based on a religion, but upon which religion will the state be based. Falwell realizes that the nation will be guided by some type of an ethical system, but he objects that the national secular ethic has become too divorced from the insight and the anchoring strength of biblical fundamentalism. While he does not object to the secular ethic which embraces religious diversity and pluralism, he insists that the basic content of the law reflect biblical law. Thus Falwell can tolerate religious pluralism as long as fundamentalist values are shared by the diverse nation.

In conjunction with this connection between law and religion, Falwell also has a different historical understanding of the separation of church and state, which was a reaction against the establishment of a tax-supported state church of England.

> Our Founding Fathers sought to avoid this favoritism [church supported by taxpayers] by separating church and state in function. This does not mean they intended a government devoid of God or of the guidance found in scripture.... The establishment of a state religion such as that which was established in England, the Church of England, and severing the relationship between God and government are two entirely different matters. Our Founding Fathers most certainly did not intend the separation of God and government.[8]

The wall between church and state should therefore stand for the separation of the institutional church and institutional state, but it does not require removing values based on religion from being an integral component of society.

This confidence in the belief that government should not be separated from God results in the confrontation of the modern debate over the role sacred ethics should play in the development of the national secular ethic. Falwell proclaims his right to use his influence for the support of religious laws. He defends his right by explaining that

> If a labor union in America has the right to organize and improve its working conditions, then I believe that the churches and the

pastors, the priests and the rabbis of America have a responsibility, not just the right, to see to it that the moral climate and conscience of Americans is such that this nation can be healed inwardly. If it is healed inwardly, then it will heal itself outwardly.[9]

For Falwell, if American greatness is predicated on biblical faithfulness and if the American political system encourages groups to organize in order to effectively express their views, then organizing people who believe in the secular efficacy of a sacred ethic is quite proper. Although the legitimacy of religious influence in politics and law is controversial, it is the result of different answers to much deeper questions of the role of the Bible and the source of American greatness. Falwell can support his programs by stressing the American religious heritage and the right of all to be involved in the political process. The critical issue in evaluating Falwell is how a single, religious perspective, biblical fundamentalism, can be broad enough to relevantly speak to a widely diverse populace. What does Falwell do with American pluralism, which was the major factor behind the emphasis upon American law in secular, nonsacred terms as outlined in the section on Connecticut law?

Falwell recognizes that America is a pluralistic and diverse country. Falwell's emphasis, like Ellul's emphasis on a precise theological understanding of the role of religion in government, makes it very difficult to maintain religious freedom and respect of other faiths which legitimately disagree with Falwell's, and Ellul's, formulation. Falwell respects religious diversity in saying that

> Doctrinal difference is a distinctive feature of a democracy. Our freedoms have given us the privilege and the luxury of theological disagreement. I would not for a moment encourage anyone to water down his distinctive beliefs. But we must face realistically the fact that there are Christians in the world today who have lost the luxury of disagreement. When the entire issue of Christian survival is at stake, we must be willing to band together on at least the major moral issues of the day.[10]

Falwell begs at least two questions, questions which are of extraordinary importance for the modern debate. First, Falwell recognizes the religiousness of secular humanism, but does not respect those who are religious who share humanistic values. Protestant thought that incorporates some Calvinist type of sanctification doctrine, and certainly traditional Catholic thought, views human ability to improve oneself as part of human responsibility to God, not as a self-centered religion. Their approach may lead to agreements with humanistic tendencies centering on human activity that accepts the wisdom of the Bible without accepting the Bible literally. By naming humanism as one of the five great national sins, he eliminates humanism from being a contributing constituent to the development of a secular ethic. Falwell is so concerned with the necessity of restoring a secular ethic based on a sacred ethic that he ignores the fact that to have a secular ethic based on a sacred ethic requires a general agreement on this sacred ethic itself, while he eliminates the positive influence that a Christian humanism can provide.

Quite closely associated with this difficulty is his insistence that Christians must band together on "at least the major moral issues of the day." But his definition of the moral issues automatically precludes banding together by Christians. Not only is there sincere, legitimate disagreement among faithful Christians on matters such as abortion, homosexuality, and the fractured family, there is certainly disagreement on humanism, which many sincere Christians embrace. Falwell asks for Christians to agree with him on his understanding of the major moral issues of the day. He is asking for an acceptance of a sacred ethic that can only be had on agreeable grounds other than what he requires.

The primary difficulty with Falwell's analysis is that it boils down to an either/or choice. Either one agrees with the literal interpretation of the Bible, or one does not understand the source of American greatness or the reason for its alleged decay. Falwell's analysis is completely dependent upon this literal interpretation, and while many of his other points may be quite useful in understanding contemporary America, he creates an analysis that illustrates the difficulty of relating sacred and secular ethics.

As both Berman and Ellul argued, law is most effective when it expresses a societal value which had broad consensus. The consensus springs from the people as it expresses their deeply felt values. These values cannot be imposed in a democratic society.

A sacred ethic like Falwell's can regain its secular influence only by convincing free people of its legitimacy. Laws that attempt to enforce the sacred ethic without secular consensus will be effective only with coercive enforcement. Laws that express sacred values in secular terms and with secular reasoning may be effective as it was in Tapping Reeve's and Zephania Swift's Connecticut and as Falwell showed among the non-Christian founders of America. However, paying lip service to religious pluralism while insisting on a sacred ethic agenda of national renewal to be had in the mechanics of biblical literalism reverses the American solution of Swift, Reeve, and the founders in using the wisdom of the sacred ethic to teach the secular ethic. To be successful, and probably to be faithful, American sacred ethics must show secular society the wisdom and efficacy of morality. Sacred ethics will not be successful, and probably not faithful, if it must impose morality.

Falwell does an excellent job in explaining that the United States has adopted a secular ethic—humanism—that has become divorced from much of the traditional Christian heritage of the country. This secular ethic, a religion itself, rightly needs to be characterized as a religion and dealt with as such. Concurrently, he has an excellent point in arguing that the abandonment of values has left the United States with broken families and promiscuity. He is also quite American in insisting that he and fellow religious leaders have a perfect right to influence the return of the country to a more moral climate.

The problem, however, lies in the fact that such a return must be on the basis of a basic societal agreement on what is right and wrong, and on what is an appropriate way of life. This basic consensus of what the secular ethic should be, or to what degree a sacred ethic should play in developing the secular ethic, depends not upon unilateral insistence of the acceptance of a very narrow and specific theological principle, but by learning from various principles in order to find deeper meaning upon which agreement can be reached. For instance, one can argue that abortion is wrong from a biblical perspective. One can also argue against abortion from a perspective which states that it is psychologically damaging to the mother, as well as noting that humans would think that there is something wrong with any nonhuman species that regularly aborts its children. All of these arguments can be promoted without government intervention to prohibit abortion by persuading the public that there are logical justifications for respecting and accepting a sacred ethic's wisdom of at least limiting abortion. This approach does not challenge a woman's right to an abortion, but teaches why abortion can be a poor choice. Thus, instead of requiring the literal interpretation of the Bible, it may be more helpful to distill the wisdom of the Bible and complement it with modern approaches in order to transfer the sacred principles into supportable secular ways of life.

By relying exclusively on this narrow interpretation of finding God's will, Falwell runs the risk of imposing the sacred ethic that runs the risk of moral tyranny, an event that will generally result in the popular rejection of the sacred ethic, instead of using the sacred ethic to teach, influence, and inform the secular ethic. While Falwell insists that all he is doing is exercising his constitutional right to influence government by freedom of action, his radical insistence on literalism — a sacred ethic — can only become secular through coercive government enforcement. Therefore, while Falwell provides an insight that the American secular ethic is a religiously flavored value system, his solution fails to bridge the differences of religiously diverse America. In order to bridge this pluralism, the sacred ethic, instead of coercing morality, must justify its morality in terms that speak to diverse Americans.

10. Mario Cuomo and the Moderate Traditionalists

While conservative Christians like Jerry Falwell have received great publicity and attention, a second group of Christians and non-Christians have begun to speak about law, politics, church, and religion. This is a group that is frightened by any attempt to tie American society to a single religious set of values, even if they strongly support the values of a single religious group. One of the most articulate spokesmen of this group is Mario Cuomo. Cuomo's best known statement of his understanding of religion and law is his 1984 speech at the University of Notre Dame, and the analysis of this speech is the subject of this chapter.

There are three major concerns of Cuomo. First he is concerned over a recent lack of respect given to the idea of the separation of church and state. Second, he distinguishes religious belief from public morality. Third, he attempts to define his role as a politician within the Catholic church. While many of Cuomo's concerns are tied to particular problems that arise within Catholicism, they are illustrative of the problems of blending and separating religion and law.

Cuomo's speech was given in light of the influence of Falwell and the Catholic hierarchy's position on abortion. Both actively spoke in favor of using religious belief in the political sphere, particularly in regard to the abortion question. Cuomo is clearly uncomfortable with the idea that powerful religious groups or individuals should have a major influence on law, and he either does not grasp or he rejects the notion that public morality (secular ethics) has a strong religious content.

Cuomo is worried that religious leaders do not honor the idea of the separation of church and state.

> Certainly, although everybody talks about a wall of separation between church and state, I've seen religious leaders scale that wall with all the dexterity of olympic athletes. In fact, I've seen so many candidates in churches and synagogues that I think we should change election day from Tuesdays to Saturdays and Sundays.[1]

Cuomo obviously feels that fundamentalist Christians like Falwell have bridged the traditional wall of separation of church and state. It is important to note that the starting point for Cuomo's argument is the relation of church and state rather than law and religion. Cuomo falls victim to the mistake of the economic historians by generally equating religion with church and law with the state. Because of this initial move, he argues past Falwell because he has missed Falwell's insight that the laws of the nation can be and have been founded on religious principles, whether or not laws are explicitly founded on the church. While Cuomo seems to dislike the sight of candidates in religious places, his key issue is the difference between religious belief of the individual and the church contrasted with the public morality by which the country is governed.

The central problem for Cuomo is that an elected leader is in deep conflict by attempting to remain loyal to his individual beliefs and simultaneously follow and enforce a public morality with which he may not agree. He confronts the classic problem of attempting to choose between sacred ethics and secular ethics. In Cuomo's words

> The Catholic public official lives the political truth most Catholics through most of American history have accepted and insisted on: the truth that to assure our freedom we must allow others the same freedom, even if occasionally it produces conduct by them which we would hold to be sinful.[2]

If the matter were this simple, others could merely be allowed to be freely sinful, and there would not necessarily be any damage to the faithful politician. But the problem fully reveals itself, and Cuomo implicitly recognizes it in his abortion stand, when it is realized that one must enforce a secular ethic which makes one's own self sinful. The problem is further complicated if one follows a biblical perspective which concentrates on the faithfulness of a people rather than the very recent notion of concentrating on the faithfulness of the individual. While Cuomo's abortion stand will be taken up more fully, it is worth noting here that Cuomo supports the necessity of following a secular ethic even when it conflicts with a sacred ethic.

It would seem that Cuomo would agree with Berman and Ellul that law is effective and legitimate when it is based on values that have a consensus of societal support. Berman and Ellul felt that law, when springing from societal intuitions or from spontaneous belief, provided the most stable, worthy law, and similarly, Cuomo states that

> Our public morality, then—the moral standards we maintain for everyone, not just the ones we insist on in our private lives— depends on a consensus view of right and wrong. The values derived from religious belief will not—and should not—be accepted as part of the public morality unless they are shared by the pluralistic community at large, by consensus.[3]

Cuomo goes on to explain that many agnostics joined the civil rights movement even though that movement was for decades nurtured in the black churches. And he further says that those who are on the political left are not upset by their alliance with religious people who oppose hunger, the arms race, and exploitation. His point is simply that there are occasions when the values of the religious and the a-religious coincide and that only when they coincide should they be allowed to direct the government, a point which Falwell similarly makes in his description of America's founding fathers. The difference is the degree of influence the religious person should use in order to persuade others that the ethics have secular validity.

If we are not to allow religious belief to guide the country as it would with Falwell, what is its role for Cuomo? Cuomo responds that because each of us is free to express our religion, each of us is

free to argue for a government policy of a nuclear freeze, for a
state ban on contraceptives, and for a law prohibiting abortion.
Each of us can do so, not because all America should have identical
religious beliefs, but because each may feel that our country would
be a better country if these policies were enacted.[4] But then Cuomo
asks if attempting to influence others by promoting one's religious
values, even on the basis of persuasive argument, is really helpful,
essential to human dignity; or whether it threatens the ability to
function as a diverse, pluralistic community.[5] Cuomo radicalizes
the choices provided to a politician when he asks

> I believe that I have a salvific mission as a Catholic. Does that mean
> I am in conscience required to do everything I can as Governor to
> translate all my religious values into the laws and regulations of the
> State of New York or the United States? Or be branded as a
> hypocrite if I don't?[6]

Cuomo continues to his final difficulty of his relation to his
church and the roles of the leaders of his church. He believes that
prelates and politicians should not be tied too closely together. He
protests the fact that there is room for disagreement in other matters within the church, even in church/state matters, but there is
none in abortion. He notes that many who endorse abortion are
not a "ruthless, callous alliance of anti-Christians," so that opposition to someone on moral grounds does not automatically make
one become an evil person.[7] He also explains

> that legal interdictions of abortion by either the federal government
> or the individual states is not a plausible possibility and even if it
> could be obtained, it wouldn't work. Given present attitudes, it
> would be "Prohibition" revisited, legislating what couldn't be en-
> forced and in the process creating a disrespect for law in gen-
> eral.[8]

Thus even though Cuomo believes that abortion is wrong, he feels
that it is not his duty to enforce his own sacred ethic on the
people.

There is very much to admire in Cuomo's approach. Cuomo
is quite correct in recognizing the difference between religious

belief (sacred ethics) and public morality (secular ethics). A lawmaker in a democratic, pluralistic society certainly has the responsibility to develop and enforce laws that promote peace, harmony, stability and other values which the secular society holds. He cannot simply impose his catechism on the public, because of its constitutional inappropriateness and because of the disrespect that it would engender toward both law and religion. The sacred ethic must not be imposed on the secular ethic, for as Ellul noted, the spontaneous natural law is not something that can be imposed, but must come from the society.

Cuomo is also quite correct in questioning whether the promotion of one's religious beliefs should be done if it ruins the harmony needed among diverse religions in a pluralistic society. Cuomo does not have to search long through history to find instances where the dogmatic insistence upon a single religious perspective has radically changed a country. One only need look at Iran or Ireland to see the results of religious extremism. Cuomo certainly fears that the fundamentalist conservatives, often including many Catholics, are on a course which insists exclusively on a single religious perspective which could lead to an ugly fractionalization of a widely diverse America. It was precisely this type of fractionalization which the Connecticut justices overcame by moving jurisprudence to a scientific, reasoning process which expressed societal values without relying upon religious sanction for a decision. So Cuomo certainly has justification in arguing against religious extremism that attempts to impose a sacred ethic without consensual support, and he has justification in fearing religious debate which becomes so fractionalizing that it drives people away from consensus-building ethics to defensive, privatized ethics.

There are, however, at least four problems with Cuomo's approach. First, his understanding of law is too restrictive. Second, he fails to recognize the possibility of sacred ethics providing a special knowledge which society needs. Third, he too narrowly restricts freedom of speech. Fourth, he ignores the need for the preservation of historical values.

Cuomo suggests a notion that law comes from government; this notion is too narrow. If law is secular ethics, then law is a way for diverse society to order lives, create a stable and peaceful society, make sense out of existence, and order civilization. These ethics are not limited to acts of the legislature or executive pronouncements, but are a product of these governmental factors as well as custom, belief, societal intuitions and spontaneous agreement of what is right and wrong in society. It is a mistake for people to expect government to create laws which solve societal problems when those problems are more appropriately and effectively solved by laws outside of the governmental sphere. However, Cuomo does not recognize these other types of law and consequently seems to give up on allowing religious influence in law. For Cuomo, looking at law emanating from the state and religion emanating for the church, there is great reason to fear the association of the two. However, if one realizes that law and religion exist as ethics apart from their most commonly perceived institutional manifestations, one can see that the assistance secular ethics and sacred ethics can give to one another can help each without inaugurating church-dominated state or state-dominated religion. By not recognizing the subtler level of ethics in law, Cuomo confines law and religion to a level where the only meeting place can be a detrimental one.

The second problem is that Cuomo seems to fail to acknowledge that religion has useful sources of knowledge which other parts of society lack. While secular society creates ethics on the basis of what is practical along with shared philosophical and sometimes metaphysical assumptions, religion is the part of society which acknowledges access to spiritual life. Whether or not one believes that people see visions and dream dreams, those initially spiritual visions and dreams can be translated into secular wisdom by persuasive argument. Martin Luther King, Jr., stands as a prime example of a man who spiritually believed the goodness of treating blacks and white equally, and he was able to transfer that wisdom to non–Christians to create a secular civil rights movement.

Secular ethics in the United States have been heavily dependent upon the wisdom of sacred ethics. The ideas of the Protestant Code described by Albanese, the jurisprudence of the Connecticut Supreme Court justices, the importance of the individual emphasized by Luther, and the values of the importance of human life are but a few of the values religion has helped teach to secular society. Considering the influence of sacred ethics, one must remember that a long history exists of exactly this type of teaching influence not only in classrooms or pulpits, but in economics, civil rights, and the Constitution. While sacred ethics need not dictate law, they do have a role in providing the wisdom for secular life.

Relatedly, Cuomo restricts the notion of free speech on behalf of sacred ethics. Cuomo is concerned that religious persuasion may harm social harmony, and in extreme and violent forms he is certainly correct. However, the exchange of religious ideas is also a marvelously fertile opportunity for new insights and growth which can help both sacred and secular ethics. Just as Cuomo should not restrict the wisdom inherent in sacred ethics, so he also should not prevent the improvement of religion and law by restricting the vigorous exchange of religious ideas.

The best check against the rise of an extremism radical enough to destroy the societal harmony necessary for a democratic society is to allow religious and nonreligious arguments to be fully aired before an educated and informed society. Demagoguery and radicalism are most successful when there are no significant ideas to combat them. Whether by lack of education (as in many third world countries), suppression of expression (as in Iran under both the Shah and Khomeini, and in czarist and communist Russia), or historical animosity inhibiting useful interchanges of ideas (as in Ireland and the Middle East), it is the lack of interchange that is harmful. Unlike these situations, the United States has a history of provocative and useful interchanges which are not always bloodless, but are far advanced over these other situations. Restricting debate is dangerous, because of the danger of the unchecked strength of the current secular ethic.

Finally, the secular ethic must continually be critically examined. As the Connecticut justices realized, it is necessary to express values in terms people can understand, discuss, reject, modify, and accept. It is also necessary to respect the values of the past, not simply because of sentimental attachment, but because they are already expressions of societal wisdom of how to deal with life. While such wisdom is not infallible and may become anachronistic, it should not be rejected without careful thought. Cuomo deeply respects this aspect of the Catholic tradition, but he also needs to respect Falwell's point that many of the values upon which this country was founded, values shared by both Falwell and Cuomo, are wise values which should not be driven out of modern America without great thought. He also fails to come to terms with Falwell's valid point that America is run by a secular humanism, a value system which must be open to criticism. One cannot use the fear of church-state relations to divert attention from questioning whether secular humanism is an ethic which truly represents the consensual ethic of Americans, or whether it has become dominant because of the lack of critical evaluation. Cuomo confronts a valid fear of church dominance of government, but fails to allow sacred wisdom to ligitimately criticize secular humanism.

Cuomo does an excellent job in recognizing that pluralistic America must base its laws on consensual agreement. The secular ethic is not something which can be identical to a sacred ethic unless the society is religiously homogenous like ancient Israel or early Connecticut. He is probably correct in warning that religious debate may lead to an unwanted disruption of the needed social harmony. He is quite American in insisting that the church be kept out of state functions.

However, Cuomo wraps up the argument in simple institutional fears which do not account for the wisdom of a sacred ethic in civil rights (even though Cuomo uses civil rights as an example of the agreement of Christians and non–Christians) and he seems to fear vigorous free speech. While Cuomo argues that he is appropriately separating religion and law, he is sewing seeds for an equally dangerous, noncritical acceptance of the secular ethic.

Cuomo has made an impressive and important beginning in understanding the role of religious belief and public morality and he accurately portrays the problem of allowing the church to dominate state affairs. But he, like many others, too narrowly defines both law and religion so that he does not account for the special wisdom that sacred ethics may provide. He also neglects to adequately consider the importance of historial values provided throughout American history by the wisdom of sacred ethics. His restrictive fear of promoting religious values, while understandable, is itself counterproductive.

11. Ethics in Contemporary America

Both sacred and secular ethics are under attack in these modern debates. American secular ethics are being attacked by sacred ethics that ask why the secular ethic has left out the sacred. Drawing upon a theology incorporating American history, conservative fundamentalists feel that their isolation harms their own rights and harms the country. There is a great deal of legitimacy in this concern as well as some overreaction.

It is clear that many of the "moral" laws which were conspicuous at the founding of the country no longer exist. Sexual laws, blue laws, and acknowledgement of dependence upon divine will are rare and there is less explicit grounding of laws upon religious texts. If Falwell is correct in giving biblical roots to free enterprise, competition, and business ambition, then there has been a drift away from these biblical values toward a more socialized welfare state. Religious texts are excluded from classrooms to an unprecedented degree in American history, and Falwell's literal interpretation of the Bible is not shared by many in the country. So conservative fundamentalists certainly have reason to feel that secular ethics have bypassed them.

At the same time, the secular ethic in the United States remains heavily dependent upon inherited religious wisdom. As Berman explained, the notion of fair trials has a religious base. The sanctity of the individual and of human life certainly owe a great deal to religious wisdom. Laws encouraging economic development were wedded to the Calvinist understanding that success in business would be a sign of God's favor. Laws prohibiting stealing and killing, statutes prohibiting incest and making adultery grounds for divorce, and bedrock values allowing criticism of government certainly have parallels in the Bible. So while there should be legitimate concern over some of the trends of our society, there also should be the realization that many legislators are similar to the people Falwell identified as our founders who were not necessarily Christians, but who drafted laws dependent upon biblical wisdom.

The conservative fundamentalists have made a positive contribution in making the secular ethic accountable. Attempts to pass off laws as being purely scientific, economic, or humanitarian fail because, even in the seemingly innocuous laws, there are decisions about who we are as people and why we value the things that we do. It is important to question the values expressed by the secular ethic and to understand them as values so that Americans can knowledgeably consider whether those values are the values they want to live by. It is important to realize that there is an existentialism of practical self-realization and science in our schools, not because these things are necessarily bad, but so Americans can understand exactly what is being taught to their children and so that the sacred ethics can dialogue with these things instead of condemning them or passing by them.

Sacred ethics are under counterattack by the secular ethic which insists that law be religion-free. The moderate traditionalists argue that religion is potentially too divisive, as seen in Ireland and Iran, to be used in debate. Further, attempts to impose a specific religious ethic on society must be firmly rejected as a violation of church and state separation. As with the fundamentalists, there is both legitimacy in the traditionalist position as well as overreaction.

Clearly, religion is a powerful, life-centering phenomena that can produce disastrous consequences in political debate, and equally, a great source of pluralistic America's success is attributable to keeping the institutional church out of the state. Cuomo and his supporters have good reason to question whether or not Falwell's biblical literalism is an appropriate guide for diverse America. And their objection to a fundamentalist attitude which often lumps opponents into groups of evildoers is certainly consistent with the need to discourage disharmony.

At the same time, the secular ethic should be accountable for the values it promotes. Secular ethics are not value-free, and attempts to explain laws as neutral are only deceiving. Laws may be neutral in the sense that they do not choose between competing religions, but they are not neutral in the sense that they are not based on values. Those values must come from somewhere and they require evaluation.

Americans must create a method that respects and learns from the wisdom of the sacred ethic and incorporates the wisdom into a workable secular ethic. For example, when religious diversity confronted Connecticut justices like Zephania Swift and Tapping Reeve they turned to a rational, written, logical explanation of the reasoning of their judicial decisions, decisions that generally perpetuated the religious truths of the state's history, but within a context which gave all an opportunity to examine the reasons. Leaders like Cuomo must now translate the insights of their sacred experience into practical, rational explanations of its existential efficacy.

The argument of whether the Moral Majority will be victorious may be misplaced. Falwell rejects existentialism as being a-religious. But, if a sacred ethic can show that not only is it wise for metaphysical reasons, but because there is practical, daily wisdom that helps both religious and a-religious, then there is an opportunity for a sacred ethic to engraft its morality onto a secular ethic in terms acceptable to society. For instance, a sacred ethic that discourages sexual promiscuity cannot only draw upon biblical condemnation of fornication, but can argue that there are health and psychological reasons for avoiding promiscuity. These health and psychological reasons may well be accepted by many who reject the Bible. By accepting the nonbiblical reasoning, a secular ethic may be formed which reflects the content of the sacred ethic and may create a more trusting attitude toward the sacred ethic itself. The solution is not Falwell's return to the literal interpretation of the Bible, nor is it to Cuomo's willingness to exclude religion from the debate. It is for sacred ethics to translate its wisdom into values which obtain secular endorsement.

Conclusion

From a philosophical and practical standpoint, law and religion are completely interdependent. Both are ethical attempts to order life and make sense of all that surrounds us. Drawing on its sacred and metaphysical resources as well as its daily pragmatics, religion provides morality. Drawing on its existential wisdom as well as borrowing from philosophical and religious systems, law provides an ethic which expresses a way of life for a society more diverse than a denomination. Both efforts are attempts of expressing the outlines of a way of life by showing the important values by which we live. Thus, the common American approach of identifying religion with church and law with state is too constricting. The institutional church and the institutional state are both powerful organizations seeking at least to perpetuate themselves, if not control their constituents. Law and religion are deeper efforts to provide the ethics expressing society's values.

Philosophical analysis, such as provided by Berman and Ellul, provides excellent insight into the connection of law and religion, although both limit their analysis. Berman identifies the connection primarily in terms of their shared symbols of ritual, tradition, authority, and universality of concepts. Law and religion share these symbols and have been historically interdependent, but the interdependence does not merge the two. For Berman, law remains a process of determining responsibilities and rights of society and religion remains society's understanding of the ultimate purpose of life. Without religion's wisdom, law loses its relevance. Berman's analysis effectively illustrates the interdependence of structures and beliefs, but needs to be clarified to show that secular law needs the legal component of structures and the religious intuition of purpose just as religion needs the same legal and religious component. This difficulty is solved by understanding each as an ethic which needs the legal and the religious elements as defined by Berman. Berman also leaves open the question of how his analysis applies to a religiously diverse society in which the religious intuitions of various denominations will conflict, making the structures difficult to create.

Ellul, operating from a strict theological premise, claims that law develops from religion. At its best, law is a natural law that spontaneously springs from the people as part of their intuitively felt values. It is when humans objectify and study law that it ceases to be effective. Moreover, Ellul argues that law is actually a justice enacted by God, that justice being Jesus Christ. Jesus was God's act of forgiveness and mercy and all law is to be judged in comparison to Jesus. Ellul argues from a theological perspective that has little relevance to humans because it ignores the role of human responsibility and the positive value of rationality. His Christocentricism makes it difficult to provide a basis for diverse denominationalism because the Christology is itself debatable in a Christian forum as well as being objectionable to non-Christian elements of society. The insistence upon the theological perspective somewhat arrogantly bypasses non-Christian humanity. The concept of sacred ethics recognizes the role of such theological wisdom while secular ethics recognizes the need to address values held by all humanity within society.

Thus, from a philosophical perspective, the connection of law and religion must be understood as a broad process of making sense out of life through religious and legal means. The concepts of sacred and secular ethics respect the distinguishing roles of law and religion while linking their shared purpose.

The identification of religion with church and law with state has led many historians to incorrectly describe American legal history. Economic historians such as Nelson, Friedman, and Hurst claim that America was initially a religiously guided country as evidenced by numerous "morality" laws. However, near the time of the American Revolution, the country became more interested in economics. Consequently, these historians claim that all laws should be analyzed on their economic content. The economic historians make the mistaken assumption that religion no longer influenced the law, but what these historians miss is the adaptation of religious values that classified business success, ambition, and hard work as godly virtues. Thus, religion did not cease to be important, but its focus changed to values which cannot simply be equated with the institutional church. The economic historians' mistaken assumption excludes religion and provides a false understanding of the development of American law.

However, contemporary debates over the operative values show that noneconomic values are important in American law. To be surprised that such a debate occurs, or to claim that it is inappropriate is to admit that one has not recognized the values in law through American history. A more correct view understands law as a complex value development based on religious principles, economics, and politics, such as the theory of Presser, and contributes to a more accurate understanding of American law. The concepts of sacred and secular ethics recognize that the values motivating law are this complex mixture of diverse motivations which order society.

The example of Connecticut legal history does not prove the judicial connection of law and religion, but it is suggestive that such a connection has existed and may well be duplicated. Both Swift and Reeve held strong theological beliefs which influenced their jurisprudence. That jurisprudence, however, was an attempt to teach and perpetuate the sacred wisdom of Puritan Connecticut in a language and a manner which was secularly appropriate for a society no longer strictly Puritan. Reeve and Swift clearly valued the wisdom of their religious past, but they also understood the need to speak to a diverse state, and modified the traditional sacred language into an ethic with secular appeal. The study of Swift and Reeve suggests that sacred ethics need not be abandoned in developing the secular ethic, and neither must the sacred ethic or secular ethic control the other. Connecticut's approach was a healthy dialogue between the sacred and the secular.

Falwell and Cuomo and their counterparts make this a timely book. Both the fundamentalists and the moderate traditionalists struggle with the role religion should play in the public sphere.

Falwell demands a return to a nation guided by biblical values and biblical literalism. Cuomo demands an absolute wall between church and state so that no one's religious freedom is curtailed. Falwell astutely recognizes that some value system will dominate society, that the value system must be open to criticism, and that religion is an important resource to use in creating the secular ethic; however, his solution demands an abandonment of any sacred ethic which conflicts with his own sacred ethic. Cuomo appropriately recognizes that in diverse America, a sacred ethic cannot be imposed on all people, that a distinction must be made between religious belief and public morality, and that the secular ethics recognizes the valuable role religion can play, as it did in the civil rights movement, without necessitating church controlled law.

This book has not meant to be authoritative. It is perhaps impossible to prove the exact interaction of law and religion in a rational presentation just as it is perhaps impossible to prove the existence of God in a rational presentation. This book has meant to be suggestive of the thought that law and religion are connected in ways that are often overlooked to society's detriment. By correcting the philosophical basis, the dialogue between religion and law can be accurately observed. This correction reveals some pitfalls of past analysis and the example of the Connecticut judges shows how the two can interact in a subtle but productive manner. Addressing the connection does not require violent confrontation, nor intolerant rejection, but can, and must be, addressed in a thoughtful, productive manner. It is my hope that this book stimulate not only scholarly examination of the philosophical and historical connection of law and religion, but that it also attempt to bring some initial suggestions for frameworks in which the important debates of the values of America be conducted in the political sphere without vindictive, judgmental, or bitter attitudes. The history of the United States has been to respect the legitimacy of sacred ethics and to integrate them into a secular ethic which is composed of substantive, important values unifying a diverse country. Hopefully, this book will assist in the continuation of that history.

Chapter Notes

Chapter 1

1. Harold Berman, *The Interaction of Law and Religion*, 11.
2. Ibid., 12.
3. Ibid., 24.
4. Ibid., 33.
5. Ibid., 34, 36.
6. Ibid., 29.
7. Ibid., 40.
8. Ibid., 47.
9. Ibid., 56, 58, 59.
10. Ibid., 54.
11. Ibid., 62-63.
12. Ibid., 64-65.
13. Ibid., 67.
14. Ibid., 52.
15. Ibid., 68, 69.
16. Ibid., 83.
17. Ibid., 84.
18. Ibid., 88-89.

Chapter 2

1. Jacques Ellul, *The Theological Foundation of Law*, 11.
2. Ibid., 10.
3. Ibid., 18, 19.
4. Ibid., 37, 39-43.
5. Ibid., 87.
6. Ibid., 105.

Chapter 4

1. Catherine L. Albanese, *American Religions and Religion*, 252–258.
2. Ibid., 285.
3. Ibid., 250.

Chapter 5

1. William E. Nelson, *Americanization of the Common Law*, 1–6.
2. Ibid., 6.
3. Ibid., 37–39.
4. Ibid., 37.
5. Ibid., 20–21.
6. Ibid., 13–14.
7. Ibid., 46–51.
8. Ibid., 54–62.
9. Ibid., 147–158.
10. Ibid., 164.
11. Ibid., 131–136.
12. Stephen B. Presser, "'Legal History' or the History of Law: A Primer on Bringing the Past into the Present," *Vanderbilt Law Review* 35: 858.
13. Lawrence M. Friedman, *A History of American Law*, 14–15.
14. Ibid., 32, 33, 37, 45.
15. Ibid., 48.
16. Everett C. Goodwin, *The Magistracy Rediscovered: Connecticut 1636–1818*.
17. Friedman, 49–51.
18. Ibid., 161.
19. Timothy L. Fort, "A Jurisprudence of Faith: An Experiment in Using Theology to Interpret Jurisprudence," *The Catholic Lawyer*.
20. Grant Gilmore, *The Ages of American Law*, 9.
21. Friedman, 409–418.
22. Ibid., 464, 472.
23. Ibid., 435, 475, 511.
24. James Willard Hurst, *Law and the Conditions of Freedom*, 5–6.
25. Ibid., 12, 28–29.
26. Ibid., 29.
27. Albanese, 2.
28. Morton J. Horwitz, *The Transformation of American Law 1780–1860*, 7–8, 17, 19–22.
29. Ibid., 254.
30. See e.g., A.W.B. Simpson, "The Horwitz Thesis and the History of Contracts," *University of Chicago Law Review* 46: 533.

31. Richard A. Posner, *Economic Analysis of Law*, 7.

32. Ibid., 102.

33. Ibid., 103.

34. Stephen B. Presser and Jamil S. Zainaldin, *Law and American History*, xvii.

35. Ibid., xviii.

36. Stephen B. Presser, "'Judicial Ajax': John Thompson Nixon and the Federal Courts of New Jersey in the Late Nineteenth Century," *NWL Rev.* 76:423.

37. Presser, "Legal History," 863–866.

Chapter 6

1. Dwight Loomis and J. Gilbert Calhoun, ed. *A Judicial and Civil History of Connecticut*, 9.

2. Mary Jeanne Anderson Jones, *Congregational Commonwealth, Connecticut, 1636–1662*, 70–71.

3. Everett C. Goodwin, *The Magistracy Rediscovered: Connecticut 1636–1818*, 37–45.

4. Ibid., 39–49.

5. Anson Phelps Stokes, *Church and State in the United States*, 410.

6. Goen, *Revivalism and Separation in New England*, 13.

7. Gaustad, *The Great Awakening* . . . , 16.

8. Ibid., 110.

9. Gaustad, *The Great Awakening* . . . , 117–120.

10. Richard J. Purcell, *Connecticut in Transition, 1775–1818*, 92.

11. Ibid., 97, 318–319.

12. Charles Roy Keller, *The Second Great Awakening in Connecticut*, 13–24.

13. Herbert Parker, *Courts and Lawyers of New England*, vol. III, 627.

14. Purcell, 347–349.

15. Ibid., 376.

16. Keller, 3.

17. Keller, 111, 145; Purcell, 32–33.

18. William Warren Sweet, *Religion in the Development of American Culture: 1765–1840*, 200.

19. Loomis, 143.

Chapter 7

1. Eleanor P. Swanson, *Tapping Reeve: American Law Pioneer*, 24.

2. Hon. David S. Boardman, "Sketches of the Early Lights of the Litchfield Bar," in Kilbourne, *The Bench and Bar of Litchfield County, 1709–1909*, 42.

3. Milton Lomask, *Aaron Burr: The Conspiracy and Years of Exile, 1805–1836*, 371.

4. Swanson, 8, 24.

5. Tapping Reeve letter to Sally Adams quoted in Swanson, 24.

6. Tapping Reeve, *The Sixth of August*, 4.

7. Ibid., 4.

8. Swanson, 24.

9. Tapping Reeve, *The Sixth of August*, 5.

10. Samuel Church, *Litchfield County Centennial Celebration*, 54.

11. 1 Conn. Rep. 13.

12. 1 Conn. Rep. 39.

13. Reeve, *Law of Baron and Femme*, 33.

14. Ibid., 286–287.

15. Ibid., 202.

Chapter 8

1. Loomis, 177; Morse, 69.

2. Swift quoted in Simeon E. Baldwin, "Zephania Swift," in William Draper Lewis, ed., *Great American Lawyers*, vol. II, 108.

3. Zephania Swift, *System of the Laws of the State of Connecticut*, 322.

4. John Calvin, *Institutes of the Christian Religion*, vol. I, translated by Henry Beveridge, 43.

5. Zephania Swift, *Correspondent*, 130.

6. Calvin, vol. II, 37.

7. Swift, *Correspondent*, 129–130.

8. Swift, *Digest of the Laws of the State of Connecticut*, 24–25.

9. Swift, *Correspondent*, 119.

10. Ibid., 17.

11. Ibid., 125.

12. Swift, *Vindication of the Calling of the Special Superior Court . . . for the Trial of Peter Lung*, 5.

13. Ibid., 4–21.

14. Ibid., 22–24.

15. Ibid., 27–34.

16. Ibid., 37.

17. Ibid., 39–48.

18. Ibid., 40.

19. Ibid., 45.

20. Swift, *Digest of the Laws . . .*, 10.

21. 2 Conn. Rep. 40.

22. 2 Conn. Rep. 541.

23. 2 Conn. Rep. 40, 43.

24. Ibid.

25. 2 Conn. Rep. 40, 45.

26. Swift, *System of the Laws* . . . , 320.
27. Swift, *Digest of the Law of Evidence* . . . , 47.
28. Ibid., 49.

Chapter 9

1. Jerry Falwell, *Listen America*, 13–14.
2. Ibid., 25.
3. Ibid., 12.
4. Ibid., 14–15.
5. Ibid., 45, Quoting *Webster's Second Collegiate Dictionary*.
6. Ibid., 178.
7. Ibid., 178.
8. Ibid., 46.
9. Ibid., 17.
10. Ibid., 225.

Chapter 10

1. "Religious Belief and Public Morality: A Catholic Governor's Perspective," speech given September 13, 1984, 1. (From speech's text.)
2. Ibid., 4.
3. Ibid., 7.
4. Ibid., 5.
5. Ibid., 6.
6. Ibid., 6.
7. Ibid., 10.
8. Ibid., 13.

Bibliography

Ahlstrom, Sydney E. *A Religious History of the American People*. New Haven, Conn.: Yale University Press, 1972.

Ahlstrom's book provided a general background of American religious history. While a small part of the book was helpful in understanding Connecticut specifically, the book was more useful in deepening basic historical knowledge. Ahlstrom's book is basically concerned with the history of Protestant development largely because these denominations were the dominant forces of early America. Ahlstrom gives considerable detailed attention to descriptions of the early American denominations. His book is geared toward geographic demographic facts as well as analysis of the motivating theologies for each denomination. Although Ahlstrom's approach has been challenged (as by the next entry in this bibliography) because it focuses on Protestant history to the exclusion of minority denominations, his book remains the best, comprehensive treatment of American religious history. It is highly recommended both to a beginning reader of religious history as well as to the trained theologian.

Albanese, Catherine L. *American Religions and Religion*. Belmont, Calif.: Wadsworth Publishing, 1981.

This book was primarily useful for sketching the American Protestant Code. Albanese divides the book into two parts: one part analyzes the general religion of America, a religion of the powerful which is indebted to the Protestant Code. The second part argues that there are many other religions in America, such as American Indian religions and American Judaism. This second part (like this book on law and religion) is more suggestive than conclusive, but still makes excellent reading. This is an excellent book for obtaining a general overview for understanding the basic analysis of American religion as well as the complexity of diverse America. It should, however, be read in conjunction with other standard analyses, like the previously described Ahlstrom book in order to truly appreciate the diversity Albanese introduces.

Bainton, Roland H. *The Age of Reformation*. New York: D. Van Nostrand, 1956.

Bainton's book sketches the philosophical and historical elements of the Protestant Reformation. While his historical treatment is good, his treatment of the theological tenets of the Reformers is the strength of the book. In particular, he has an excellent analysis of John Calvin. The trained theologian may prefer to work directly with Calvin's original sources; Bainton's book is a very good place for the jurisprudential scholar to gain an introduction to Calvinist thought.

Baldwin, Simeon E. "Zephania Swift," in *Great American Lawyers*, ed. William Draper Lewis. Philadelphia: John C. Winston, 1907.

Baldwin provided an introductory analysis of the life and philosophy of Zephania Swift. Like most secondary sources, Baldwin's analysis of Swift should not be relied upon exclusively, particularly when many original sources exist. Nevertheless, for a scholar who wants to address the life of Swift, this essay will frame the important events and themes of Swift's life and jurisprudence.

Beecher, Lyman. *A Sermon Preached at the Funeral of the Hon. Tapping Reeve*. Litchfield, Conn.: S.S. Smith, 1827.

This funeral oration was an important source of information for understanding Tapping Reeve. Beecher was highly flattering of Reeve, and argued that Reeve's religion made a huge difference in his life. Care should be taken in studying this or other funeral speeches since there is a natural tendency to focus only upon an exaggerated opinion of the deceased's best qualities. In Reeve's case, this fear is somewhat reduced because Beecher's description is substantiated by other descriptions. This speech, therefore, is a good start on any analysis of Reeve, and is better than most secondary sources.

Berman, Harold J. *The Interaction of Law and Religion*. New York: Abingdon Press, 1974.

For anyone beginning the study of law and religion, this should be a starting point. Berman is recognized as one of the most knowledgeable scholars in the field and this is his basic statement of his theory. Since Part One of *Law and Religion* spends a great deal of time considering this book, I would refer the reader to that text.

_____. *Law and Revolution*. Cambridge, Mass.: Harvard University Press, 1983.

This extremely complex and somewhat tedious book should be read by those who have a very substantial interest in the field of law and religion. The basic thesis of the book, that modern Western legal systems were formed in reaction to and are heavily indebted to the

Papal Revolution is rather startling, but extremely well argued. Berman goes into exceptional detail to show the relationship of church law and secular law in individual fields, such as manorial law, feudal law, property law, etc. This thesis continues along the theme that there is a direct, concrete relationship between the church and state laws in the content of substantive law.

Blawie, James and Marilyn Blawie. "The Inherent Right to Local Self-Government in Connecticut." *Connecticut Bar Journal* 30: 231, 1956.
This article sketched some of the governmental developments of early Connecticut. The article would be useful for individuals studying early Connecticut history, local self-government, or for added depth into the Connecticut history. It is an article that would really be useful for a scholar interested in these specific areas.

Boardman, David S. *Sketches of the Early Lights of the Litchfield Bar*. Litchfield, Conn.: 1860.
This was a marvelous little book that gave general biographical sketches of famous Connecticut lawyers. It is centered on graduates from Litchfield's law school, the first in America, organized by Tapping Reeve. The book certainly is not a deeply detailed description of the early Connecticut lawyers, but it is an excellent starting point for identifying significant men in Connecticut jurisprudence.

Calvin, John. *Institutes of the Christian Religion*, trans. Henry Beveridge. Grand Rapids, Mich.: Wm. B. Eerdmans, 1981.

_____. *On God and Political Duty*. ed. John T. McNeill. Indianapolis, Ind: Bobbs-Merrill, 1950.
McNeill's book is a presentation of Calvin's themes of the relationship of God to government, the people to government in light of their duty to God, and the people's ultimate duty to God. McNeill's book effectively isolates these important themes, which are direct excerpts from Calvin's works. It is a good book to work into the direct reading of Calvin's *Institutes*. The *Institutes* was Calvin's seminal work. It is a theological classic and worthy of the reader's attention simply on that basis. It is also worthwhile because it was so vital for the establishment of early American government.

Church, Samuel. Historical Address. Pittsfield, Mass.: Chickering and Extell, Steam, Block and Job Printers, 1876.

_____. *Litchfield County Centennial Celebration*. Hartford, Conn.: Edwin Hunt, 1851.
This material was not included in the text, but I would highly recommend these two speeches by another pre–Civil War Con-

necticut justice. Church learned well the lessons taught by Tapping Reeve and Zephania Swift. He made religious tolerance into a religious creed of ultimate importance. Similarly, and not coincidentally, Church also praised the development of scientific jurisprudence with a heavy reliance upon respect of precedent. He therefore continued to enforce the wisdom of the Puritan past in the language and methodology of scientific jurisprudence.

Cohn, Henry S. "Connecticut's Divorce Mechanism: 1636–1966." *American Journal of Legal History* 14: 35, 1970.

This is another specialized article, concerning the history of divorce law in Connecticut. Unfortunately, the article can only give a cursory treatment of the subject. It does not add much to the present study, but it may be for a more targeted study emphasizing divorce law.

Cuomo, Mario. *Religious Belief and Public Morality: A Catholic Governor's Perspective.* Given at University of Notre Dame, Terre Haute, Ind., September 13, 1984.

This speech, given at the University of Notre Dame, is one of the most articulate presentations of the questions that must be asked in studying religion and politics. Cuomo's purpose seems to have been to raise the sophistication of the debate, and it seems to accomplish that objective. Cuomo's answers to the questions he poses seem to be rather tentative, but his purpose is not to make conclusive answers. A more specific analysis of the strengths and weaknesses of Cuomo's arguments is contained in the text.

Daggett, David. *Argument Before the General Assembly of State of Commonwealth.* New Haven, Conn.: Oliver Steele, 1804.

_____. *Count the Cost: An Address to the People of Connecticut.* Hartford, Conn.: Hudson and Goodwin, 1804.

_____. *Facts Are Stubborn Things or Nine Plain Questions to the People of Connecticut.* Hartford, Conn.: Hudson and Goodwin, 1803.

_____. *Steady Habits Vindicated or a Serious Remonstrance to the People of Connecticut Against Changing Their Government.* Hartford, Conn.: Hudson and Goodwin, 1805.

_____. "Sun Beams May Be Extracted from Cucumbers, but the Process Is Tedious." In *American Forum*, eds. Ernest J. Wrage and Barnet Baskerville. New York: Harper, 1960.

Like Samuel Church, David Daggett was another pre–Civil War Connecticut justice. Daggett wrote prolifically, and these sources are excellent and quite entertaining speeches. Daggett seemed to venerate

religion more than the other Connecticut justices, except for Reeve.
But he apparently had little direct participation with the church. He
attended services primarily to study the oratory of the minister. He
was an extremely controversial man, with a long political career
prior to his appointment to the Supreme Court. For a scholar interested in studying original material of early Connecticut justices,
Daggett's works are an excellent place to begin.

Dulles, Avery. *Models of the Church.* Garden City, N.Y.: Image, 1974.
    This book has become standard reading for almost every theology
student. Dulles breaks the notion of church into five different types
and shows the different concerns for each type. His method is effective for showing that the concept of church has more than one meaning. Specifically, it is useful in showing that an institutional concept
of the church is only one possible alternative. This would be a good
resource both for those interested in theology as well as for non-
theologians who want to broaden their religious sophistication.

Dutton, Henry. *A Revision of Swift's Digest of the Laws of Connecticut.* New
    Haven, Conn.: Henry S. Beck, 1871.
    This revision actually did not add anything to the analysis of Swift,
but it was instructive in revealing that Swift's jurisprudence remained influential in Connecticut for a long period of time. If an edi-
tion of Swift's original *Digest* is unavailable, this would be closely indicative of the original work.

Dutton, Samuel W.S. "Address of Rev. Samuel W.S. Dutton at the
    Funeral of David Daggett." *Connecticut Reports* 20: vii.
    Like Beecher's funeral oration for Reeve, Dutton's funeral speech
should also be viewed somewhat cynically. It is useful as an
embellishment on Daggett's life, but should not be relied upon too
heavily.

Ellul, Jacques. *The Theological Foundation of Law,* trans. Marguerite
    Wieser. Garden City, N.Y.: Doubleday, 1960.
    Ellul's book is an excellent analysis of the relationship of law and
religion, and should be read by anyone who has an interest in this
field.

Falwell, Jerry. *Listen America.* New York: Bantam Books and Doubleday
    Publishing, 1980.
    Falwell's book is analyzed more thoroughly in the final section of
this book. His book is probably the best starting point for understanding the perspective of many fundamentalist Christians. I would
strongly recommend this book so that a reader is able to see Falwell's
total theology instead of relying on news media excerpts.

Flaherty, David J., ed. *Essays in the History of Early American Law*. Chapel Hill, N.C.: University of North Carolina Press, 1969.

_____. "The Use of Early American Court Records in Historical Research." *Law Library Journal* 54: 342, 1976.
Flaherty's books are good starting places for legal research. *Essays* give an overview of scholarship in legal history, and indicate the methods used by legal historians. The article treats the use of historical records, giving rather basic, commonsense tips which may be helpful to the beginning investigator, but will be well known to the experienced scholar.

Forgeus, Elizabeth. *The History of the Storrs Lectureship in the Yale Law School*. New Haven, Conn.: Yale University Press, 1940.
Forgeus sketches this influential lecture series at Yale. As with the other Connecticut sources, it will really be useful to someone who is doing serious research in Connecticut law. Within Connecticut history, this book is another tool to identify the activities of relevant, influential people. From there, the scholar can choose the individuals of interest, and examine their original works.

Friedman, Lawrence. *A History of American Law*. New York: Simon and Schuster, 1973.
Friedman's book is also dealt with more extensively in the second section. His book remains the best source for a comprehensive treatment of American legal history. Friedman certainly ascribes to the economic theory which remains the dominant theory of legal historians. This is a "must read" book for anyone with an interest in American legal history.

Gaustad, Edwin Scott. *A Religious History of America*. New York: Harper and Row, 1966.

_____. *The Great Awakening in New England*. Glouchester, Mass.: Peter Smith, 1965.
Gaustad is one of the very best religious historians in the country. His *Religious History*, assisted by many photographs, does not go into the tremendous detail Ahlstrom's book provides. Rather, it is a bit more general, but the generality does not compromise the analysis of American religious history. This book, along with Albanese's book, are superb for initial readings in religious history, and are good books even if one is familiar with American religious history. The *Great Awakening* book is a much more detailed account of the Great Awakening. His and the Goen book give a very solid description of the Great Awakening.

Gilmore, Grant. *Ages of American Law*. New Haven, Conn.: Yale University Press, 1977.
This book, originally given as the Storrs Lecture Series, breaks American legal history into ages of discovery, faith, and anxiety. Gilmore does not go into historical detail, but instead articulates the broad themes of American history. This is an excellent book, and should be read by anyone interested in legal history.

Goen, C.C. *Revivalism and Separatism in New England, 1740–1800*. New Haven, Conn., and London: Yale University Press, 1962.
As mentioned above, Goen's book along with Gaustad's provides a very solid description of the Great Awakening. Goen concentrates on the recurring revivalism to the turn of the century. I would highly recommend this to anyone with an interest in American history.

Goodwin, Everett C. *The Magistracy Rediscovered: Connecticut 1636–1818*. Ann Arbor, Mich.: UMI Research Press, 1981.
This is simply a terrific book and should be read by anyone with an interest in religion and law. Goodwin looks at how the Fundamental Orders of Connecticut were based directly on Calvinist notions and guided Connecticut government. He continues his analysis up to the 1818 Constitution of Connecticut, showing that religious underpinnings both continued and were altered as government became more complex. Although he does not always consider how changing religion impacted on the changing law, his book is an excellent thought provoker and is very highly recommended.

Hauerwas, Stanley. *Vision and Virtue*. Notre Dame, Ind.: Fides, 1974.
This is one of many Hauerwas books that explains ethics as a product of our communities. He argues that ethics are our everyday habits which are formed by communities. Communities should therefore strive to be faithful communities building individual character, a character that will act out good habits. Hauerwas is sometimes difficult to read, but his philosophy is excellent and is highly recommended to anyone.

Hicks, Frederick C. *Yale Law School: The Founders*. New Haven, Conn.: Yale University Press, 1935.

————. *Yale Law School: From the Founders to Dutton, 1845–1864*. New Haven, Conn.: Yale University Press, 1936.
Hicks' books provided additional background material for Connecticut law and also provided quite a bit of analysis of the philosophy of David Daggett, another Connecticut justice referred to in this bibliography.

Holden, Benedict M., Jr. "Freedom of Expression in Connecticut." *Connecticut Bar Journal* 29: 240, 1955.

This brief article about the legal development of free speech in Connecticut is well written, and would be useful insofar as the value of free speech is perceived to be a "religious" value for Americans. It was not, however, an article which was used, except for background purposes, in this book.

Horwitz, Morton. "Historical Foundations of Modern Contract Law." *Harvard Law Review* 87: 917, 1974.

_____. *The Transformation of American Law: 1780–1860.* Cambridge, Mass., and London: Harvard University Press, 1977.

Horwitz is considered in Part II of this book. Suffice it to say that Horwitz has received enormous attention for his book, and any student of legal history would be well advised to study Horwitz's theory that the development of nineteenth century law was due to an alliance of the judiciary with the new, emerging merchant class.

Hurst, James Willard. *Law and the Conditions of Freedom in the Nineteenth Century United States.* Madison, Wis.: University of Wisconsin Press, 1956.

_____. *The Growth of American Law.* Boston: Little, Brown, 1950.

Hurst also is considered in Part II. His works are also of great influence in American legal history, particularly as he persuasively argues that economic development was the motivating force behind nineteenth century law. This also is a "must read" book for anyone interested in legal history.

Jones, Mary Jeanne Anderson. *Congregational Commonwealth: Connecticut, 1636–1662.* Middletown, Conn.: Wesleyan University Press, 1968.

Jones' book is limited in time and scope, since it only considers the first twenty-six years of Connecticut history. But what she does analyze, she analyzes well. She particularly examines the religious influence on early Connecticut law. Most of her remarks can be found in other sources, but for detail in early Connecticut law, her book is very good.

Keller, Charles Roy. *The Second Great Awakening in Connecticut.* New Haven, Conn.: Yale University Press, 1942.

This book is also limited in scope, but it was a very important book. It was the primary book for analyses of the "quiet revivals" of post–Constitution Connecticut featuring revivalists like Lyman Beecher. Obviously, one must have an interest in Connecticut history in order to find this book as useful as I found it, but if that interest exists, this is a valuable monograph.

Kilbourne, Dwight C. *The Bench and Bar of Litchfield County, 1709–1909.* Litchfield, Conn.: 1909.

This is the best source to obtain an initial, short biographical sketch of Connecticut judges. The book is not designed to rigorously analyze each justice, but it generally gives enough information about each judge to give the scholar enough information to decide whether a particular justice might be worth investigating.

Kung, Hans. *Does God Exist?* New York: Vintage Books, 1981.

This may appear to be a strange inclusion; however, I would strongly recommend it to any serious reader. Many of its pages are devoted to an evaluation of theories critical of Christianity such as the theories of Freud, Feuerbach, Nietzche, and Marx. Although tedious, it provides a basis for reasonable Christian belief in God, which ultimately is the core to any reasonable Christian integration of religion and law. While the reader may disagree with Kung's conclusion, it is a superb example of a responsible Christian attempt to deal with the modern world.

Lewis, Leon P. "The Development of a Common Law System in Connecticut." *Connecticut Bar Journal* 27: 419, 1953.

This was a generalized article indicating the religious and legal sources for Connecticut's common law system. Its analysis is not objectionable, but it does not attempt extensive conceptual integration of the sources of the common law.

Lomask, Milton. *Aaron Burr: The Conspiracy and Years of Exile 1805–1836.* New York: Farrar, Straus, Giroux, 1982.

Read almost by default, this book is an interesting book on Burr, but was useful for my book because it contained some material concerning the relationship of Burr to Tapping Reeve.

Loomis, Dwight and Calhoun, J. Gilbert, eds. *Judicial and Civil History of Connecticut.* Boston: The Boston History Company, 1895.

This book is still the most comprehensive treatment of Connecticut legal history. It outlines the state's legal history, and does a fair job of integrating that history with civil history. It also provides some very helpful biographic data on Connecticut jurists.

McBrien, Richard P. *Catholicism.* Minneapolis, Minn.: Winston Press, 1980.

This is the best reference work on Catholicism available. McBrien covers nearly everything one could think of in crisp, direct analysis. Although his work was not heavily used for my book, his book would be very useful for anyone researching anything that may relate to Catholicism.

MacDonald, Herbert S. "An Obituary Note on the Connecticut Justice of the Peace." *Connecticut Bar Journal* 35: 411, 1951.

This was a specialized piece, like Maltbie's article, that helped to orient the researcher, but provided little help for the issue of law and religion.

Maguire, Daniel C. *The Moral Choice*. New York: Doubleday, 1978.

Maguire's book indicates that ethics are not simple matters of right and wrong and further, that the sources useful in analyzing moral choices vary. Thus there are different sources of knowledge applying varying degrees to different kinds of choices. This is a well written and provocative book which should be read by anyone interested either in law or religion.

Maltbie, William M., "The Courts and Constitutions of Connecticut." *Connecticut Bar Journal* 9: 269, 1935.

This was another article of general description of Connecticut legal structure that was helpful for orientation purposes, but not for any distinctive analysis.

Morse, Jarvis Means. *A Neglected Period of Connecticut History: 1818–1850*. New Haven, Conn.: Yale University Press, 1933.

This was a vitally important book on post–Constitution Connecticut. Morse details the political and economic history of the state and sketches the religious development. Morse does little integration of religion with economics and politics, but his work is the best place to begin if one is considering early nineteenth century Connecticut.

National Conference of Catholic Bishops. *The Challenge of Peace*. Washington, D.C.: United States Catholic Conference, 1983.

This book significantly contributes to the modern debate of religion and law, not because it makes the debate an issue, but because it makes political arguments from a religious perspective. This is an extremely well nuanced argument concerning nuclear armaments and is very good reading either from a strictly political viewpoint or from a purely theological perspective.

Nehum, Milton and Schultz, Louis M. "The Grand Jury in Connecticut." *Connecticut Bar Journal* 5: 111, 1931.

Another specialized article of Connecticut legal history which is important mostly on a regional level.

Nelson, William Edward. *Americanization of the Common Law: Impact of Change on Massachusetts Society, 1760–1830*. Cambridge, Mass.: Harvard University Press, 1975.

This extremely important book on legal history is considered in the text. Although it focuses on Massachusetts history, it is an influential book beyond this state. Nelson also made some initial attempts to understand the influence of religion on legal development.

Niebuhr, Richard. *Christ and Culture*. New York: Harper and Row, 1951.
Like Dulles' *Models of the Church*, this book has become a standard text for theology students. It develops different ways of looking at the role Christ played and the role used by Christians to associate with or disassociate from society. Like Dulles, it is very helpful in revealing the complexities of theologies instead of limiting religion to one standard role. This book may be slightly more useful to the theologian than the jurist, but it would be a helpful book for both.

Olin, John T., ed. *A Reformation Debate*. Grand Rapids, Mich.: Baker Book House, 1966.
This book printed a Reformation debate between Calvin and Saldeto. While the debate does not impact the religion-law issue, Olin's introductory remarks were helpful in highlighting the major points of Calvinism. It is another good way for the nontheologian to ease into Calvinism.

Osbourne, Norris Galphin, ed. *History of Connecticut in Monographic Form, Volume III*. New York: The State History Company, 1925.
While this book provides a history of Connecticut, other sources such as Loomis, Purcell, and Morse are much better for research.

Parker, Herbert. *Courts and Lawyers of New England, Volume III*. New York: The American Historical Society, Inc., 1931.
Parker sketches the courts of New England in much the way others in this bibliography sketched Connecticut judges. This is another useful book to identify interesting judges.

Peeters, Samuel. *General History of Connecticut*. 1781.
This is an extremely biased narrative of Connecticut history written prior to the nineteenth century. Peeters, a disgruntled clergyman, is so extreme that his history has little objective descriptive value. However, the book is extremely entertaining and does reveal the degree of emotion provoked by the religious-legal questions of early Connecticut.

Posner, Richard. *Economic Analysis of Law*. Boston: Little, Brown, 1972.
Posner has become an extremely influential thinker and judge on contemporary jurisprudence. He strenuously argues that the best tool for legal analysis is economics. Posner's philosophy has numerous points of opposition to this book on religion and law. It

is, however, an important book highly recommended to any scholar in the field.

Presser, Stephen B. "Judicial Ajax: John Thompson Nixon and the Federal Courts of New Jersey in the Late Nineteenth Century." *Northwestern University Law Review* 76: 423, 1981.

_____. "'Legal History' or the History of Law: A Primer on Bringing the Law's Past into the Present." *Vanderbilt Law Review* 35: 849, 1982.
    Presser is a contemporary scholar who is worth considerable attention. The Nixon article specifically analyzes the jurisprudence of a particular judge and uses the judge's religion as a contributing factor to his jurisprudence. This concern for understanding the importance of religion is broadened and underscored by the legal history article which argues that humans are interested in values apart from their economic connections. The book, *Law and American History*, is the first casebook of legal history and emphasizes the need to examine individuals and movements instead of simply stereotyping institutions. All of these sources are highly recommended.

_____, and Zainaldin, Jamil S. *Law and American History*. St. Paul, Minn.: West Publishing, 1980.

Purcell, Richard J. *Connecticut in Transition, 1775–1818*. Washington, D.C.: American Historical Association, 1918.
    This is the best history for Connecticut from the American Revolution to the Connecticut Constitution. It contains an excellent bibliography for further reading. This is a prime starting place for anyone interested in studying early Connecticut.

Reese, W.L. *Dictionary of Philosophy and Religion: Eastern and Western Thought*. Atlantic Highlands, N.J.: Humanities Press, 1980.
    A useful reference book of past and present theology and philosophy.

Reeve, Tapping. *Law of Baron and Femme*. New Haven, Conn: Oliver Steele, 1816.

_____. *The Sixth of August or the Litchfield Festival*. Hartford, Conn.: Hudson and Goodwin, 1806.
    These were the primary sources for the study of Tapping Reeve. The thrust of their philosophy is considered in the text.

_____. *A Treatise on the Law of Descents in the Several United States of America*. New York: Collins and Hannoy, 1825.

Reuschlein, Harold Gill. *Jurisprudence — Its American Prophets: A Survey of Taught Jurisprudence.* Westport, Conn.: Greenwood Press, 1951.
Reuschlein studies important scholars and presents their theories. It is a moderately useful book for jurisprudential students.

Root, Jesse. "Introduction to Root's Reports," I *Root* ii.
Root's reports catalogued Connecticut cases. The introduction was a good summary and analysis of Connecticut law through the eyes of an early nineteenth century observer. His analysis does not add anything particularly novel, but it is a decent summary.

Santos, Hubert, J. "The Birth of a Liberal State: Connecticut's Fundamental Orders." *Connecticut Law Review* 1: 386, 1968.
This is one of several articles describing the 1636 Connecticut Constitution. The Shipman article, below, is more useful, but this Santos article is a good general description of the document.

Sejdwick, Charles F. *Fifty Years of the Litchfield County Bar: A Lecture Delivered Before the Litchfield County Bar.* 1870.
Another work on the Litchfield bar added somewhat to other works on the same subject.

Shipman, Arthur L. "Connecticut's First Lawyer." *Connecticut Bar Journal* 1, 1927.
This was a very useful article on Roger Ludlow. Ludlow, the first Connecticut lawyer, drafted the Fundamental Orders. The article also tries to explain the relationship of Ludlow to Rev. Thomas Hooker, who provided the theology for the Fundamental Orders. This article is recommended for anyone interested in the law-religion field, and in Connecticut history.

Simpson, A.W.B. "The Horwitz Thesis and the History of Contracts." *University of Chicago Law Review* 46: 533, 1979.
This influential article severely criticized the Morton Horwitz thesis of legal history. It would be good to read this in conjunction with the Horwitz book.

Stokes, Anson Phelps. *Church and State in the United States.* New York: Harper, 1950.
This seminal work was a useful reference work for setting the stage of church-state relationship in Connecticut.

Swanson, Eleanor P. *Tapping Reeve: American Law Pioneer.* 1966.
This book was very valuable in studying Reeve. Swanson quotes original sources and provides an excellent analysis of Reeve. This book assists the reader in understanding Reeve and in guiding the reader to original sources.

Sweet, William Warren. *Religion in the Development of American Culture: 1765–1840*. New York: Charles Scribner's Sons, 1952.
This book examined the impact of religion in America. It has been criticized as being overly concerned with the impact of powerful religions at the expense of being sensitive to other faiths.

Swift, Zephania. *Address to the Rev. Moses C. Welch*. Windham, Conn.: John Byrne, 1794.

_____. *Correspondent*. Windham, Conn.: John Byrne, 1793.

_____. *Digest of the Law of Evidence in Courland Criminal Cases and a Treatise on Bills of Exchange and Promissory Notes*. Hartford, Conn.: Oliver D. Cocke, 1810.

_____. *Digest of the Laws of the State of Connecticut in Two Volumes*. New Haven, Conn: S. Concruse, 1822.

_____. Letter to John Fitch. May 26, 1800.

_____. Letter to Joseph Isham. December 2, 1794.

_____. *System of the Laws of the State of Connecticut*. Windham, Conn.: John Byrne, 1796.

_____. *Vindication of the Calling of the Special Superior Court . . . For the Trial of Peter Lung*. Windham, Conn.: John Byrne, 1796.
These works were the primary material for examining Zephania Swift. They are considered more fully in the text.

Tuchman, Barbara. *The March of Folly*. New York: Alfred A. Knopf, 1984.
Tuchman analyzes why governments insist upon pursuing paths which are contradictory to their own self-interest. As part of this analysis, Tuchman describes the Renaissance popes whose sordid morality and oppressive power contributed to the Protestant Reformation. It provides a useful example of the mistake of identifying a religion with its institutional representative.

Index